BLACK PEARLS
for
PARENTS

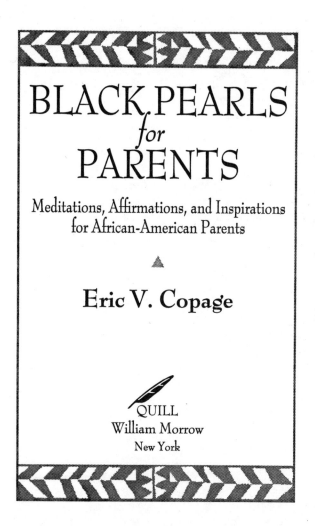

BLACK PEARLS
for
PARENTS

Meditations, Affirmations, and Inspirations
for African-American Parents

Eric V. Copage

QUILL
William Morrow
New York

Grateful acknowledgment is made for the use of material from *My Soul Looks Back, 'Less I Forget: A Collection of Quotations by People of Color*, compiled and edited by Dorothy Riley, HarperCollins Publishers. Copyright © 1993 by Dorothy Winbush Riley.

It is the policy of William Morrow and Company, Inc., and its imprints and affiliates, recognizing the importance of preserving what has been written, to print the books we publish on acid-free paper, and we exert our best efforts to that end.

Library of Congress Cataloging-in-Publication Data

Copage, Eric V.
    Black pearls for parents : meditations, affirmations, and inspirations for African-American parents / Eric V. Copage.
        p.   cm.
    Includes index.
    ISBN 0-688-13098-4
    1. Parenting—Religious aspects.   2. Afro-American parents—Prayer-books and devotions—English.   3. Meditations.   I. Title.
BV4529.C66   1995
242'.6—dc20   94-33073
                                                        CIP

Printed in the United States of America

4   5   6   7   8   9   10

BOOK DESIGN BY MICHAEL MENDELSOHN/MM DESIGN 2000, INC.

To my father, John E. Copage,
whom I respect, admire, and love

INTRODUCTION

I became a black man on April 10, 1987. I remember the date because it is the birthday of my first child, my son Evan. His birth intensified questions I had been asking myself for a lifetime, and the need finally to answer those questions transformed me and made me whole. Specifically, I wondered, "What does it mean to be a black person? What does a black person stand for? And what values of our culture shall we pass on?"

Those questions seem especially important for many reasons. America is changing, as is the world, and it is no secret that black America—regardless of class, economic status, or ideology—is in crisis. The choices we make today and the values by which we live will determine the status and power of our people in the new millennium.

So, on the eve of my son's birth I wondered, What values would allow him to prosper in this brave new world? What would help him survive the vicissitudes of ideological fads and his own evolving personal attitudes? I reflected on the upbringing of accomplished black people and noticed that their parents instilled what I call a muscular black pride—a pride born not only of rhetoric, but of concrete constructive actions. I saw that the parents of those children regularly reaffirmed their love for their offspring, and made their children feel at once special, and yet part of the larger human enterprise. *Black Pearls for Parents* is modeled on the advice and deeds of those parents.

In the everyday whir of housekeeping, making a living, and dealing with the myriad demands of life, it's easy, even for the most conscientious of parents, to allow the daily process of raising children to become a blur. *Black Pearls for Parents* is a daily reminder to help bring that process back into focus. And while this book is targeted to black parents, it is meant for all African-American adults, for we are all custodians of the next generation. Whatever our biological link to black children, all of us are their role models, their teachers, their mentors, their guardians.

Parent or not, you needn't be shy about letting the youngster around you know you are reading this book. In fact, some of exercises are meant to be done in tandem with the youngster, while others are meant to ignite conversation between adult and child. Still others, however, are more personal, and address the adult's needs. Regardless, sharing this book with your child sends the message that books are valuable resources.

If your child seems too young or old for a particular exercise, modify it so she can participate in the spirit of that day's thought. If you are the parent of an infant or preschooler, do the exercises yourself in preparation for the time when you can do them with your child. Or share the thoughts and exercises with a young relative or neighbor. Of course, all suggestions in this book are applicable regardless of whether a child is male or female, which is why I've alternated the gender of the child throughout the book.

To affirm our African ancestry is, above all, to affirm our humanity. Let us remind our children of that. And while life is neither fair nor easy, and obstacles are often thrown in our path, let us remind our children that life is also wondrous. Life is also sweet. But to partake fully in the wondrous sweetness of life requires discipline and vision.

Let us guide our children with our words and deeds to express the highest ideals of our traditions. Let us pray that we set a good enough example so that our children are inspired to build upon our foundation.

—Eric V. Copage

BLACK PEARLS
for
PARENTS

FAITH

*Faith can give us courage to face the
uncertainties of the future.*
—*Martin Luther King, Jr.*

Faith is, perhaps, our greatest weapon. It can keep us strong in times of stress, keep us motivated to build the kinds of lives we dream for ourselves and our families.

Yet, strange as it may seem, we are often our own worst enemies. We adopt cynical attitudes that cheat us of potential fulfillment; we abandon hope for positive change and learn to live with the inevitable bitterness. Our children suffer and, like sponges, absorb our despair.

Without question, we need to be relentless in shoring up our faith. Daily meditation and positive thinking can help. Distancing ourselves from negative individuals and actively seeking out inspiration (through self-help books and biographies, through magazines and lectures) can also fortify us. So, too, can prayer.

*On this day, I will take five minutes to talk to
my child and communicate to her the faith I have
in her and in our people.*

BLACK IDENTITY

Celebrating Kwanzaa is not an end in itself. Neither is having an African medallion swinging from your neck, wearing a kente cloth hat, or giving your children African names.
—Eric V. Copage

A fitting quote for the day after Kwanzaa, no? While our annual celebration may be over, the goals and ideals it emphasizes and engenders should help us accomplish all we have to do throughout the year. After all, our pride in being black cannot substitute for pride in our *individual* efforts and contributions.

Let us indeed draw upon our culture, our traditions, and our history to inspire us to do *our* part for ourselves, our families and our people. And not just during Kwanzaa—but all the time.

On this day, I will take five minutes to discuss with my child an item relating to black pride—kente cloth, for instance, or a family photograph—and suggest that he let that object inspire him to excellence throughout the day.

POSITIVE THINKING

*Most folks just don't know what can be done with a
little will and their own hands.*
—Gloria Naylor, from her novel Mama Day

Some folks just don't want to hear any of that positive
thinking stuff. It requires them to act, when we all know
it's much easier to complain, blame, envy, and belittle.
Maybe they tried on a "can do" attitude once; it didn't
pay off immediately, so they gave up.

We cannot be defeatists, just as we cannot raise a
new generation of defeatists. What would happen to our
people?

*On this day, I will take five minutes to talk to my child about
the successful individual—the one who doesn't mind work
and hangs in there long past the time when others have
given up.*

IMITATION

*Children learn by seeing people doing things. If all
they see are people who don't try, it's going to be
difficult for them to try.*
                                        —Faith Ringgold

Let us first tap into our family archives to pull out the
success stories that can inspire our children—and us,
too. They need not be grandiose stories to be motivat-
ing; yet, they will exemplify perseverance, diligence, integrity.

There are many books available on historical figures and contemporary achievers in all fields. There are
monthly magazines highlighting real-life stories of African American who are realizing their dreams. And, in
some of our schools, there are events such as African-
American career day, where local citizens in various professions come to share their knowledge and
inspirational stories.

*On this day, I will take time to encourage my child
to discuss her heroes—large and small,
famous and unsung.*

HEROES

*My heroes are and were my parents. I can't see
having anyone else as my heroes.*
—Michael Jordan

We probably don't feel much like heroes most days.
We're too busy just trying to get dinner on the table on
time and to make sure our children are on the right
track. But our children watch us constantly. They see
how we handle adversity and stress; they hear our views
on life and love; and, more than anyone else in the outside world, are witnesses to our character and integrity.

We cannot simply demand our children's respect,
but must live up to it—or lose it.

*On this day, I will take time to think of three ways
I can improve my approach to life so as to inspire
my child. My everyday acts can speak
with understated heroism.*

INFLUENCES

*For most of us, keeping up with the popular culture
is one of the first things we let go. The problem is
that sometimes this lack of attention to the music
that both shapes and reflects our children makes us
miss important developments in their world, and by
extension, our own.*
— Pearl Cleage

Let's keep in touch with the television and radio sta-
tions that play such an important part in shaping our
child's world. We can listen to the groups and ask, What
are the lyrics saying? Do they glorify violence? Demean
women? While we may hate the idea of becoming the
old-fashioned parent, it is important for us to keep our
finger on the pulse of our child's entertainment, which
is to keep our finger on values being pumped into him.

*On this day, I will take five minutes to discuss with my child
his favorite entertainer. It needn't be a confrontational talk,
just a friendly chat so that
I'm aware of my child's influences and his opinion
of those influences.*

RESPONSIBILITY

> *We are responsible for the world in which we find ourselves, if only because we are the only sentient force which can change it.*
>
> —James Baldwin

Our world and our children's world are one and the same. As long as we are living and breathing, it does not do for us simply to point fingers. Nor should we throw up our hands in disgust or surrender. Rather, let us join hands with friends and allies to effect the changes we desire. To get that far, however, we must involve ourselves, be aware, show up, participate. We must learn, if necessary, to screw up our courage, ask the right questions, inject our own informed opinions, and make all worlds ours.

On this day, I will talk to my child about something he is unhappy about—it could be something at school, in her social life, or in the world at large—and help her come up with three things we can do to make the situation better.

TEMPTATION

Devil tempt but he no force.
—*Guyanese proverb*

The moment we become a parent, we take on an enormous responsibility—the care and cultivation of a human being. If the importance of leading a sober, sane, and wholesome life had never occurred to us before, it sure should kick in now.

Unfortunately, parenthood does not immunize us against our weaknesses, which run the gamut from drugs, alcohol, overeating, and smoking, to sexual temptations that can destroy our marriages and families, to mental and physical cruelty, and all sorts of other destructive behavior.

If we need help, let's get it. Let's keep the stakes in mind when the devil tempts us. Remember: Our children look up to us—let's not let them down.

On this day, I will take five minutes to look at the temptations in my life, those that threaten my family, and determine if they are in check. If not, I pledge to take immediate action to put them in check or seek appropriate help.

STYLE

Life is what your creator gave you for free. Style is what you do with it.
—Mae C. Jemison

An astronaut talking style? It may seem incongruous unless we take style in its broader sense. Style is the way we express ourselves—in what we have to say and how we say it, how we live, how we parent, how we weather disappointments, how we manage our energy and cultivate our interests. Style involves risk taking and experimentation, and so it is inextricably linked with self-confidence.

In looking at our children and ourselves, let's keep in mind that style is finding ourselves, freeing ourselves, challenging ourselves, and giving ourselves more pleasure in life.

On this day, I will take five minutes to discuss with my child the personal styles of some of his favorite people.

EDUCATION

*Education helps one cease being intimidated by
strange situations.*
—Maya Angelou

What holds some of our young people back is a feeling
of intimidation—the sense that they do not have the
stuff inside to enter the game and compete. But instead
of acknowledging their insecurities, they make excuses:
"Life is stacked against me; I'd like a chance to score,
but 'they' won't give me the ball."

We cannot underestimate the importance of an
education, which affords our children a knowledge of
themselves and a recognition of their strength and abilities. Good attendance is not enough; confidence cannot be gained by merely "showing up." Through active
involvement, our children will discover they can not
only adapt to new situations but thrive in them.

*On this day, I will take five minutes to talk to
my child about the importance of speaking up in class
and in life. For, as the lottery slogan goes—you got
to be in it to win it.*

UNCONDITIONAL LOVE

*Even though your kids will consistently do the exact
opposite of what you're telling them to do, you have
to keep loving them just as much.*
—Bill Cosby

On those occasions when our children egregiously disobey us, "loving them" is probably not uppermost in our mind. Finding a suitable punishment is, perhaps.

Ironically, it's times like these when parents need a "time-out," time to let go of the anger so that the love can bubble up again. Let's take some time to cool down if we find we're on the verge of losing control, and remind ourselves that our children will make mistakes— and it's up to us to help them learn from them.

*On this day, I pledge not to hold on to my wrath
after an appropriate expression of it. Nor will I ever
punish my child by acting like he is the greatest
disappointment in my life. I pledge to take a look at
my own anger and think about how to make
a learning situation out of a disappointment.*

EXERCISE

*Parents need to serve as role models for children and
to instill in them the fact that exercise, like healthy
eating, should be a lifelong habit.*
—Florence Griffith Joyner

Before we can become a positive role model, we have to
size up our own habits and see whether we're doing a job
that makes us proud. Perhaps we've slowed down on our
exercise goals, or we've gotten careless about our snack
habits. Let's get back on track. As for our children, we
have to be flexible. It may be that our daughter opts for
dance class instead of joining us for Saturday morning
tennis. The idea is to inspire our kids to find exercise
that excites and interests *them.*

*On this day, I will take five minutes to talk to my child about
physical exercise, and to see if we might embark on an
exercise regimen together or apart.*

January 12

SELF-CONFIDENCE

A man must believe he is somebody before he is
acknowledged as somebody.
                    —*Henry McNeal Turner*

Let's take an important step back—a *child* must believe he (or she) is somebody before he can become an adult who believes he (or she) is somebody.

Furthermore, a child must believe he is somebody special, somebody valuable, somebody with something to contribute. That means we turn down the radio to listen and talk to him; we turn off the television to read or play together; we teach him that his schoolwork is a priority, that his ideas are interesting, that his feelings warrant consideration.

The bottom line: We must believe he is somebody, and treat him accordingly, so that he, too, can believe.

On this day, I will take time to tell my child some of the
many things I respect him for.

TIME

*We don't have eternity to realize our dreams, only
the time we have here.*
                                          —Susan Taylor

Some days we look at our schedules and barely see time
in our day to brush our teeth, let alone realize our
dreams. Could be we're procrastinating by giving everyone else's needs precedence over ours. Or perhaps we
haven't allowed ourselves to figure out our dreams. We
need *our* time; it's precious, so we need to be disciplined
if we're to use it efficiently.

*On this day, I pledge to make sure to red ink some time on
my calendar for myself.*

DEVELOPMENT

*I refuse to accept the idea that the "isness" of
man's present nature makes him morally incapable
of reaching up for the "oughtness" that forever
confronts him.*
—*Martin Luther King, Jr.*

We tend to know when our excuses ring hollow. "I'm overworked and stressed out" may certainly be true, but it doesn't erase our guilt over not devoting more loving time and attention to our children. "I'm just an impatient person" doesn't excuse our yelling at them all the time.

Let's be willing to look at ourselves and figure out ways to cope with our "isness" so that we can relate to our children as we "ought" to.

On this day, I will take five minutes to talk to my child about something she would like to do, and then we will devise a way to find time to do it.

WINNING ATTITUDE

*I was the most uncoordinated kid in the world,
banging my knuckles on tables as I walked by,
knocking over lamps, two left feet on the dance floor.
I wasn't the fastest kid. I wasn't the best player.*
—Dave Winfield

Makes you wonder what ever happened to "the fastest kid" and "the best player"!

As parents, it's natural for us to want to see our child excel. But we can't be discouraged if she fails to kick the winning soccer goal, or make the advanced math class. Our child will read our disappointment and may wind up feeling like a failure and giving up.

Dave Winfield says he had to "work hard" to improve; *that* is the name of the game. It's up to us to convince our child that, if she wants something enough, she can achieve it with a diligent and focused effort.

On this day, I pledge to reenforce my child's "winning attitude" and to emphasize to her that through discipline and hard work and dedication to excellence, anyone has a shot at fulfillment.

MONEY

What we want is a little money.
—Sojourner Truth

No, money can't buy us love, but it sure makes life easier. It gives us more options and affords our children opportunities. It can enable us to live in a pleasant environment, to buy books and take classes, to travel, to go to the opera or a jazz concert, to enrich our lives and our children's lives in myriad ways. It ensures proper medical care for our loved ones and reduces our worries about the future. And it can be used to help others less fortunate than ourselves.

Not to say that making money should be our chief focus in life, nor acquiring goodies our only goal. Our children require our attention and guidance, not simply fashionable clothes and ski trips.

On this day, I will take five minutes to talk to my child about the good one can do with money: build hospitals, naming them after great leaders of our tradition; influence cultural institutions, giving charity and funding projects as we see fit. But I will also stress how values will always be more important than money.

FEAR

*The guy who takes a chance, who walks the line
between the known and unknown, who is unafraid
of failure, will succeed.*
—*Gordon Parks*

Does that mean the guy who is afraid of failure is
doomed? Not if, when faced with fear, he swallows hard
and proceeds anyway. Our children may get the unfortunate and fallacious notion that fear is there to limit
them. It is *they* who limit themselves when they allow
fear to paralyze them.

*On this day, using family, friends, or historical figures as
examples, I will take five minutes to talk to my child about
the fact that fears can in fact be surmounted. Even baby
steps forward will do it, supplying and building the confidence
necessary to take bigger and bigger strides toward success.*

PATIENCE

*Life would be so easy if we could control other
people—especially our children. It's the natural
developmental nature of children to act out and take
risks. Throwing tantrums, talking back, and
skipping school are all parts of growing up. . . .*
—Julia A. Boyd

So many times we parents end up shaking our heads
and saying, "What have I done wrong?" Well, sometimes the answer is—nothing. Not to say that certain
behavior is acceptable or ignorable. We may, in fact,
have to take action. But let's allow that our children
have things going on within themselves and in their
world that have nothing to do with the way we've been
raising them. And let's remember that a certain amount
of acting up is a regular part of growing up.

*On this day, I will make sure the lines of communication
with my child are open so that, perhaps, some of the
undesirable behavior can be avoided.*

GOOD HEALTH

*It is our duty to conserve our physical powers, our
intellectual endowments, our spiritual ideals.*
—W.E.B. DuBois

We occasionally lose sight of the fact that life constantly
throws challenges at us, puts obstacles in our paths,
trips us up in all manner of ways. Shortages of time,
money, and space tax us. Our bodies betray us with illness and disease; friends and family let us down; careers
disappoint. It is imperative that we keep ourselves
strong. When we're run-down, we cannot always summon the energy to fight. It may not be obvious now, but
our children will later come to recognize our choices and
habits as healthful ones and adopt them for themselves.

*On this day, I will take five minutes to talk to my child about
the importance of keeping our minds, bodies, and spirits
healthy, and talk about ways in which we might do that
together and separately.*

DREAMS

Nothing is achieved in a dream.
　　　　　　　　　　—Malinke proverb

Our dreams for ourselves and our children are precious, yet dreams do *no one* good if they do not compel us to realize them. Without work, our dreams can only tantalize and cause us anguish. We need to use our dreams as a tool. Daily meditation in which we vividly see ourselves accomplishing our goals can inspire us to give what it takes.

　　　Let's bury the excuses and wake up from our dreams to make them our lives.

On this day, I will take five minutes to talk to my child about one of her dreams, and coax out of her ways to make it real.

GROWTH

For me, life is all about growth.
                              —Janet Jackson

It seems we so often complain of boredom. We get stuck in routines that appear to leave no room for experimentation and play. Life can start to feel unbearably stale—nothing but unrelieved work, monotonous chores, and relentless demands by family, friends, and employers.

Perhaps we've stopped growing. We've forgotten to stretch ourselves, expose ourselves to new things and ideas, push our limits, and explore our talents.

Getting out of the rut needn't entail a major commitment of time, money, or energy. We may find fun and gratification in attending a wine-tasting class with a friend, in trying out free weights at the gym. As parents, we're entitled to some time for ourselves; it can enrich our minds, improve our bodies, and lift our spirits.

*On this day, I will take five minutes to talk
to my child about some new enterprise or area
of interest I've discovered.*

SELF-DETERMINATION

Nobody can give you freedom. Nobody can give you equality or justice or anything. If you're a man, you take it.

—Malcolm X

If you're a woman, too!

Our children must grow up with the knowledge that no person or group of people has power over them. Not white people, not a spouse or lover, not their friends, teachers, or employers. Even the child who has been diminished by an abusive or misguided parent can struggle and reclaim the dignity so unfairly robbed from him.

If, looking inside, our children do not see a quality that they would like to see, they alone have the power to install and develop that quality. No one else can give it to them, yet we *can* learn to be selective about the people we allow to come close to us, and choose only those who treat us as we deserve to be treated.

On this day, I will take five minutes to talk to my child about his own strengths and powers of self-determination.

VISUALIZATION

*I absolutely pictured myself climbing in and out of
limousines.*
                                        —Suzanne de Passe

Maybe *we* did, too—and here we are, but where's the
limo?

  We can't simply want the accoutrements of success; we have to want to *work*. Hard. We do our children
no favors if we encourage them to dream, but do not
give them the tools they will need to achieve their
dreams: discipline, tenacity, resourcefulness, a positive
mind-set.

*On this day, I will encourage my child to use her mental
images of success to inspire her to do what she can today—
and every day—to get closer to her goals.*

VALUES

The value system has been turned upside down to where in a lot of circles, if young black kids strive to get straight A's and speak proper English, they're ridiculed for being white.
—Spike Lee

It is obvious that we must "take back" our African-American value system. We start in the home, by inculcating in our children the premise that to be black is to use proper grammar, bring home A's, plan for a future, treat each other with respect. To be black is to excel and prosper.

Our history is rife with men and women of backbone, spirit, hope, and strength—people who have overcome obstacles and achieved. *That* is where our value system starts.

On this day, I will take five minutes to discuss with my child an item relating to black pride—kente cloth, for instance, or a family photograph—and suggest that he let that object inspire him to excellence throughout the day.

LOYALTY/SUPPORT

*I really do believe that every human being has
serious value. I'm in most people's corner.*
—*Elaine Brown*

Let's pause and consider: Who's in *our* corner? Do we
have friends who support and encourage our goals?
Does our mate offer a hand when we need help and a
hug when we need affection?

Whose corner are we in? Certainly our children
should be able to count on our unconditional love. Our
mate deserves the same respectful treatment we expect,
and our friends may need us to help them through times
of crisis and confusion.

*On this day, I pledge to be attuned to the emotional balance
in my household. I pledge to encourage my child, mate, or
loved one to communicate their needs to me, and I pledge to
communicate my needs to them.*

January 26

TIMING

If you criticize a boy after a defeat, it sounds like blame. When you spell out his mistakes after the team has won, he learns.
—Willie Mays

It makes sense. As adults we know that when we're down, when we're smarting from defeat, the last thing we need is someone pointing out our every fault. What a surefire way to demolish self-confidence.

On this day, I will make sure that, when I address my child, my criticism is both constructive and caring. I'll remember that timing is important.

PARENTHOOD

*It was very, very important that my sons' mother
be a mother. They wanted, needed and deserved
a mother. They didn't need an author around
the house.*

—Toni Morrison

Being constantly preoccupied with our careers while we
are with our children sends a message: My career means
more to me than you do. Yes, it's a good idea to let our
children see our dedication and industry, but let's not
carry it to the point where we do not leave a significant
portion of ourselves for our children.

Our work will sometimes engender some negative
emotions—frustration, disappointment, anger—which
we must learn to file under "job" before interacting with
our family.

*On this day, I will not turn on the TV or the radio. And I
will not do any "office" work until my child is asleep. I will
first chat with, play a game with, play catch with, bake with,
or participate in another activity with my child that requires
interaction.*

January 28

COLLECTIVE WORK AND RESPONSIBILITY

We grew up in a generation where people were concerned about what you were going to be, because the race needed you. We were reared to believe a single failure was one that we could not afford. I hope we can regain that urgency.
—Bishop Leontine Kelly

The "race" needs every one of us more than ever. We need not drive ourselves to nervous exhaustion. There are simple things we can do that take little extra effort, yet can have an impact. Next time we plan a trip to the museum with our family, invite another black child along. We can also invite other parents to join our parent groups, to come to our picnics and/or holiday celebrations. Another way of helping is to make donations to local black charities and church groups or to the UNCF. Let's figure out how we can make a difference.

On this day, my child and I will make a list of five things from which we can choose to make a positive difference for the black community so that every black person will know that we need everyone.

DISCOURAGEMENT

Gray skies are just clouds passing over.
—Duke Ellington

Not one of us is without our gray days. Our children, too, have their fair share of disappointments and difficult moments. The real danger comes when we create our own thick cloud of negativity and despair, which hangs over us day in and day out. In our gloom, we cease to recognize opportunities and the good that life has to offer.

On this day, I pledge when my children are feeling blue, to tell them they'll feel better after a good night's sleep, or urge them to look forward to summer days ahead. In other words, I will note the transitory nature of things so that they don't feel overwhelmed by bleak feelings.

EFFORT

*My Daddy used to ask us whether the teacher had
given us any homework. If we said no, he'd say,
"Well, assign yourself."*
—Marian Wright Edelman

Our child cannot get the impression that it is acceptable
to put forth the minimum required effort. Just because
the assigned homework is done, it doesn't mean the
books should be packed away till tomorrow. The next
chapter can be read, or the last chapter can be reread for
greater clarity and understanding. If division is proving
to be a challenge, then our child can work on an extra
dozen division problems.

Excellence cannot be attained when our child
only strives to meet the minimum standards. If he takes
the extra step, he will derive satisfaction from his progress and accomplishment, and this, in turn, will inspire
him to continue to work up to his ability and not just up
to the assignment.

*On this day, I pledge to get my child into good work habits
by encouraging her always to go the extra mile.*

BLACK HISTORY

*"Black Is Beautiful" of the 60's and, "I'm Black
and I'm Proud" of the 70's have not died, and are
yet applicable. For our blackness is targeted, and
ever a target. Our black history reveals a catalyst (of
faith, mostly) that has propelled so many of us to
rise above non-entity status.*
—James Thomas Jackson

A quote to welcome us into Black History Month! We
know it's here when suddenly our children are writing
reports on African-American inventors and our local library puts up a special display of books by or about no-
table African Americans.

As parents, it's entirely possible *we* can learn
something new and valuable during Black History
Month, too. The most important thing we can do, however, is make this month of tribute *work* for us by en-
suring that it is more than a change of pace at school.

*On this day, I will take five minutes to discuss Black
History Month with my child and help him draw inspiration
and motivation out of our history, and use it to fuel his
efforts to achieve his dreams.*

INTROSPECTION

*Solitude is the only answer. I need to be really alone
to do the kind of work I need to do—and be satisfied
I've done good work.*
—Jessye Norman

There are times we just have to shut the door, unplug the phone, and tell family and friends, "Sorry, no." Then, in solitude, we can fashion our dreams and goals, chart or revise our course, or just sit quietly and do nothing for a while.

Let's make sure that our time alone is *prime* time, not a few minutes squeezed in here or there, not when we're sleepy or standing over the sink or ironing board. Claiming quality time for ourselves helps prevent resentment and frustration from creeping into our relations with our loved ones, and our children will learn by our example that solitude is not to be feared, but welcomed.

*On this day, I will take at least twenty minutes to be alone
and think about my life, my goals, my dreams, and I will let
my child know that is what I am doing during my alone
time.*

ALLIANCES

*Align yourself with powerful people. Align yourself
with people that you can learn from, people who
want more out of life, people who are stretching and
searching and seeking some higher ground in life.*
—Les Brown

Elitism, or common sense? Why not open ourselves up
to those who challenge and encourage us, who introduce
us to new ideas and opportunities for enrichment? Our
children, however, may not be adept at recognizing or
handling what Les Brown calls the "energy drainers,"
people who sap our spirit and strength. To an adolescent, a negative attitude is often seen as "cool." We
need to show and teach our children how to nurture
friendships that are mutually affirmative. This doesn't
mean being snobbish—dreams and ambition transcend
income level, we already know—but smart.

*On this day, I will take five minutes to talk with my child
about distinguishing between those who say they want
success and those who will really work
to attain it.*

GOOD HABITS

*Good habits can be fine things. If you say your
prayers every night there comes a time when they
grow more meaningful to you.*
—Marian Anderson

We might condition our children to repeat the same
words of love and affirmation night after night. We
might regularly impress upon them our highest ideals
and expectations for them, and sprinkle their day with
pearls of wisdom and positive thinking, with words
meant to encourage, inspire, and motivate them. Yet we
might not see immediate results.

We have to have faith that our guidance and support are having an impact, even if it is not obvious right
now. In time our lessons become ingrained, and our
children can draw hope and comfort from the seeds we
have planted in them. It is all we can do, but at least we
will have provided them with the positive options that,
we must trust, will help them later on.

*On this day, I will take five minutes to consider whether I
am doing all I can to help my child develop
good habits in various areas.*

BOOKS

*I was unhappy for a long time, and very lonesome,
living with my grandmother. Then it was that books
began to happen to me.*
—Langston Hughes

The next time we are bored, in a funk, lonesome, or simply uninspired, let's try turning off the television and putting away the cookies, chips, and beer. Whether we are in need of a stimulus or a comforter, a passport to a new world or an explanation for this one, we can find satisfaction in the pages of a book.

As for our children, reading is simply a "must" for academic success, a means to personal growth, and a source of pleasure. Perhaps we can liven up the dinner conversation with "book talk"; it will help our children learn to articulate their opinions and just might make for a healthy bit of competition among our budding readers.

*On this day, I will read to my child or encourage her to read
a book that can interest her—a biography of a sports hero, a
book on space, doctors,
reptiles, or animals.*

PARTNERSHIP

A partner in the business will not put obstacles to it.
                                        —*Congolese proverb*

In the "business" of raising children, we and our mates must have a concurrence of thought as to what our common goals and standards are. It's possible our disciplinary methods may differ, or that what is "high-spiritedness" to one is merely rudeness to another. Perhaps one partner pushes sports while the other focuses on academics. Our being at cross-purposes can set up a difficult situation, with our child caught in the middle and possibly playing one side against the other.

On this day, I will take time to discuss with my mate our goals, frustrations, and concerns about raising our child so that we might work together more cohesively.

JOY

Life is better than death, I believe, if only because it is less boring, and because it has fresh peaches in it.
—*Alice Walker*

Fresh peaches . . . and children, too!

What a neat quote. Little things can give us such pleasure. Our children already know this; witness the joy on their faces when we present them with a favorite treat or special token, or when we take a little time to do something fun together. And what happiness that in turn gives us!

Let's open ourselves up to the things that can make us smile.

On this day, I will find something of beauty and joy in the world and share it with my child.

SIBLING RIVALRY

We were taught to be proud of each other; and we were: every good grade and victory was a family achievement. Thus, the competition never got out of hand and we were close then, and now.
                                        —James P. Comer

Sibling rivalry may seem to go with the territory, but there are ways to keep it from turning into all-out warfare. If we lavish our time and attention on, say, our oldest child, or on our only son (or daughter), we're asking for trouble. Let's strive to find a workable balance, make sure we allot one-on-one quality time for each child, and not shortchange any of our children in terms of praise and affection.

On this day, I pledge to take time to recognize each of my children's strengths and accomplishments, to resist making comparisons, and pledge to make each of our celebrations a family affair.

IDENTITY

*Blackness is not a hair style. It is not a dashiki.
Judge my blackness by the jobs that we have, by the
money we are able to generate in the community in
advance of the support services. Judge my blackness
by that.*
—Bertha Knox Gilkey

Let us cultivate in our children the idea that "blackness" is not surface, but substance. It is the power that we yield, the money that we spend, the range of choices that we have at our disposal and can afford our children.

We can't leave it up to our rap artists to weave this concept into their lyrics. It has to come from us.

*On this day, I will take five minutes to discuss with my child
an item relating to black pride—kente cloth,
for instance, or a family photograph—and suggest
that he let that object inspire him to excellence
throughout the day.*

RISK

He who is not courageous enough to take risks will
accomplish nothing in life.
—Muhammad Ali

Was there ever a time we considered taking a risk but
talked ourselves out of it? Perhaps it involved a relationship, a move, an alternate career path?

If shunning risk is holding us back from a life of
true fulfillment, we *can* do something about it. Let's
start small by rising to meet challenges rather than
turning our back on them. It's possible that one big risk
can be broken down into less frightening steps. Let's put
away the bag of automatic excuses and begin by saying
yes to one small challenge at a time.

On this day, I will pledge to help my child overcome her fears.
For an older child, I will encourage her to visualize success.
For a younger child, I will begin getting her in the habit of
taking on new things—a speaking part in the school play or
an art class—as simple ways for her to gain confidence in
meeting new challenges.

EXCELLENCE/DISCIPLINE

*Excellence is not an act but a habit. The things you
do the most are the things you will do best.*
—Marva Collins

Some of us have misunderstood. When we do not
glimpse some outstanding natural ability—in ourselves
or our children—we assume there is nothing there to be
brought out and developed. But while few people are
prodigies or geniuses, there are many enjoying rewarding careers and satisfying lives because they made hard
work a habit. In the professional world we see it again
and again, how it's the hard workers and not necessarily
the brightest or most talented who come out on top.

A determined and disciplined child will fare better
than one who has the abilities but never mines and pol-
ishes them. Discipline can be learned, and if our child
sees at an early age how an extra hour of study or practice can bring results, she will be encouraged to make it
a habit.

*On this day, I will take five minutes to talk to my child about
the importance of hard work and high standards, using
family, friends, or historical figures as examples.*

HOME

Whether you're a woman or a man, when you're out there fighting the world, you want to come home and find peace.
—John H. Clarke

When you're a child, too. A serene home environment allows us all to function at our best. It should be our refuge from stress, the place we go to nourish and nurture both our mind and body.

For our children's sake, let's commit to finding ways to manage our adult problems so they do not foul the atmosphere of our homes. Let's resist the yelling and fighting, the blaming and name-calling that hurt and worry our children.

All family members can and should be involved in maintaining the peace at home, but, as parents, we must make a deliberate effort to discuss problems and find solutions that are fair and respectful for all.

On this day, I will take five minutes to think about the stress level in my household, and, if necessary, ways to reduce that stress.

LEARNING

There are years that ask questions and years that answer.
—*Zora Neale Hurston*

Forget about bad *days;* sometimes there are bad *years!* For whatever reasons—career troubles, children's developmental stages, or a combination of the above—we might have a long stretch of particularly stressful and challenging days. This can be true also for our children, whatever their age. During those times of personal or familial stress, it can be hard to step outside of the situation and anticipate a satisfying resolution.

On this day, I will take five minutes to talk to my child about cycles—there is a season to everything—and how, with faith and perseverance, all lights will turn green.

LOVE

*Even today, when I think about my mother for any
reason, what first jumps to mind are memories of
her telling me that she loved me more than anyone
else in the world.*

—*Bill Russell*

Okay, there are going to be times that we nag and yell
and punish, but if we utter "I love you" both consistently and wholeheartedly, then that positive and reas-
suring message should prevail. This is true with our
spouses and romantic involvements as well as with our
children. But let us also put our words and feelings of
love into action.

*On this day, I will take at least five minutes to
act and respond to my child or mate with love, as well
as speak of love.*

February 14

PRIORITIES

*When I first started to write, I had no money and
slept on newspapers in an apartment. I used my
money to buy a desk and a typewriter; I had
nothing—no shelf for my books or records.*
—*Jamaica Kincaid*

What author Jamaica Kincaid did have was a desire and
a sense of priorities. She put what money she earned toward a roof over her head and the things that would
make writing possible—not designer shoes, pretty
plates, not even a bed.

It takes more than talking about becoming something, and more than wishing for it. It takes commitment. Are we doing everything possible toward realizing
our goals? Are our children? No? Perhaps we need to
figure out what's holding us all back and then find ways
to deal with that. Let's fire up our resolve and put an end
to excuses.

*On this day, I will take five minutes to discuss with my child
one of her goals, and examine with her whether she has
prioritized her life so that she might reach her goal.*

INDEPENDENCE

My parents always treated us like young adults, not kids, even when we were real little. They did that because they wanted us to be individuals, to learn how to take care of ourselves, to achieve things on our own.

—Carl Lewis

Every summer, Carl Lewis and his family traveled to visit relatives. His parents gave him and his siblings the money and had them step up to the counter to buy their own tickets. In this manner, they were taught to speak up for themselves.

As parents, we have an obligation to help our children prepare for the world.

On this day, I pledge to give my child reasonable and age-appropriate responsibilities that will simultaneously help him feel capable and give him pleasure in his independence.

February 16

WHITE PEOPLE

I feel happiness and sadness at the same time. I worry that my son is a young black man. Will his father have to explain race relations like his father did?
—Anita Baker

No doubt, we'll be talking about race relations for generations. But *how* we talk about white people and racism can have a great impact on the choices our children make with their lives.

Yes, there will be people who hate us because we are African-American. Let's not stew over *their* pathologies; it's not up to us to convince them we are worthy. Let's get about the business of planning for our future, working on our dreams, leading lives of fulfillment, seizing our moments of happiness and joy. Let's not reduce the scope of our ambitions by allegedly being "realistic" about the world, because then *we* do cede control over our lives to others.

On this day, I will take five minutes to tell my child that her life is precious, and do my best to send her into the day with a positive attitude.

RELATIONSHIPS

Avoid noxious relationships, and seek those that are nurturing.
—John E. Copage

It can be tricky when we recognize that some of the people who are closest to us are inhibiting our growth or clouding our optimism. What do we do when it's a mate, lover, parent, or best friend who brings us down?

First, let's communicate. An attack on them will just make them angry or defensive, neither of which is our purpose here. We need to calmly but unequivocally state our concerns and desires. Second, we must be committed to act; only then do we show we're serious. If our mate is in the habit of sabotaging our diet efforts, we might enlist his support by joining the Y together, or pointing out the fat content of his nightly treats and introducing a more healthful substitution.

On this day, I will take five minutes to talk to my child about the importance of communication in a relationship.

NUTRITION

When hunger gets inside you, nothing else can.
—Yoruba proverb

It is a sad fact that some of our African-American children are still going to school and to bed hungry. Still others may have contented bellies, but have merely filled up on empty calories in the form of sugar and fat.

We simply cannot have hope for our children if we neglect their crucial need for proper nutrition. Our family doctor or school nurse should be able to point us in the right direction. We can also check our local library for current magazines and books on diet and nutrition. At dinner time, in my house, my young children total the number of servings of fresh fruits and vegetables they've had during the day. A minimum of five gets them a couple of cookies after their dessert fruit. Be creative. Get your children involved early on.

On this day, I will take five minutes to discuss the importance of proper nutrition with my child, emphasizing that it will help him do better what he wants to do.

COPING

*To cheer up on those bad or frustrating days, I want
to laugh, so I watch "I Love Lucy" tapes.*
—*Gail Devers*

We all have those days we don't perform at our best—
even Olympic gold medalist runner Gail Devers. Illness,
fatigue, and stresses of all sorts sap our strength. How
do we cope? If we can find a way to cheer up, our frustrations and failures are reduced to temporary setbacks.

A bad day might be turned around after a good
workout at the gym or a walk through the park. An in-
expensive bunch of daffodils, a phone call to a supportive
friend, a funny movie, engrossing book, or a delicious
dinner can all help to buoy our spirits and cement our resolve to tackle our goals tomorrow. Let's find out what
works for us, and spare our families in the bargain.

*On this day, I will take five minutes to talk to my child
about building an arsenal of "feel good" remedies to use in
case of any temporary blues.*

February 20

INITIATIVE

*According to the commonest principles of human
action, no man will do as much for you as you will
do for yourself.*
                                        —Marcus Garvey

What this means is that our children need to learn early
on that they are their own best advocates. No one can
show better proof of their worthiness and ambition than
they themselves—by putting their own talents and intelligence into action. When the A's are on the report
card, the science fair first prize garnered, and their
names top the masthead on the school newspaper, others will be happy to speak for them, to sit with them, to
make phone calls and write letters of recommendation
for them. But first comes their own effort.

*On this day, I will take five minutes to talk to my child about
her assets and how she can achieve her goals.*

February 21

VICTORY

*Even the smallest victory is never to be taken for
granted. Each victory must be applauded, because it
is so easy not to battle at all, to just accept and call
that acceptance inevitable.*
                                        —Audre Lord

Perhaps one of the biggest mistakes we can make is neglecting to acknowledge and celebrate our little victories. Whether it's in the form of positive feedback from a teacher about our child, an enjoyable family outing to a museum, or watching the way our son reads a story to his little sister—*these* are victories! Ditto our successful efforts toward personal improvement, such as a five-pound weight loss or a commitment to read more. Our little successes tell us we are doing something right and should give us the incentive to do more.

*On this day, I will congratulate my child for some success,
no matter how small.*

SCHOOLING

I don't expect white people to educate our kids. We are responsible. The power structure will not address issues that are at the root. The challenge falls back on us.

—Gil Noble

So let us become part of the power structure. We must be present and vocal if we are to have our concerns articulated and heard. Why expect white people to spend much energy worrying about our "at risk" children, our children who spend their academic careers in remedial programs, and our test scores? There are outlets for discussion of such issues at most schools. We need to find out when and where the meetings are and show up. We can also elicit support from administrators for a special meeting for African-American parents. Perhaps there's a need for a support network for African-American parents in our community.

On this day, I will start creating an agenda, no matter how modest, for the education of all our children and begin gathering support in school and the community for that agenda.

TOLERANCE

Whenever I find myself beginning to be intolerant or insensitive with my daughters, I think back to a similar incident I put my mother through and I smile and understand their need to be themselves.
—Annette Jones White

Let's face it, children can be annoying, ridiculous, and irrational. They take to clothing we find laughable, friends we find objectionable, and postures that can drive us up a wall. It helps to stop a minute and recall *our* youth. No doubt we did our share of groping around, trying to adopt the right look and attitude. Possibly we made a few wrong turns, too. Let's refrain from losing our cool with our children. As long as their behavior is neither dangerous nor self-destructive, we can recognize it as an attempt to discover themselves and find out how they fit into the world.

On this day, I will take five minutes to think back on my childhood and adolescence, and remember some of the grief I put my parent or care giver through.

PEER PRESSURE

I always got teased. Teased about my name.
Teased about my size. I'd have to beat them up.
—Shaquille O'Neal

That teasing can be rough on a child. It can make some withdraw socially. It can make others—like Shaquille—start swinging.

What can we do to help? Some of us have children who are simply not very comfortable sharing their wounded feelings; it hurts them just to talk about things.

It might be helpful to share personal experiences from *our* childhood, which can help our child both to find appropriate methods for handling the teasing and to see that we all outgrow those things that might be embarrassing or painful to us today.

On this day, I will take five minutes to talk to
my child about any teasing or social pressure
he might be enduring and illustrate how others
have handled similar pressure.

ELDERS

*One of the problems with this country is that we're
wasting the elderly. But nature wastes nothing, so
why isn't their knowledge recycled into the children?
To me, there's nothing more wonderful than an old
person who loves children and wants to teach them.*
                                        —Eartha Kitt

We have certainly become creative at recycling everything except our most precious resource—people. Many
of our elderly still want desperately to "give," to be
treated as valued and respected members of our society.
We can begin in our African-American community by
recognizing the treasure we have in our elders and by
finding ways to invite them into our endeavors.

*On this day, I will take five minutes to discuss with my child
elderly people we respect, people we see as a repository of
wisdom. It may be a grandparent or aunt, a neighbor or a
famous person.*

KINDNESS

A good head and a good heart are always a
formidable combination.
—*Nelson Mandela*

It's easy to see how smarts count. But a good heart? Will it get our child into Harvard or Howard?

Some of us may consider that pushing fairness and compassion on our children will weaken them. How will they fare with the selfish people out there who are all too willing to take advantage of their decency?

Be cheered: A good heart is not a weak one. Quite the opposite. A good heart is strengthened by the right values, and, in truth, gives us the courage to live by what our good head is telling us. A good heart allows us to think positively instead of suspecting the worst of everyone and anticipating the futility of making an effort. Without a good heart, there is no hope and no faith.

On this day, I will take five minutes to talk to my child about the importance of developing the compassionate side as well as the analytical side of his personality.

PHYSICAL ACTIVITY

My parents had the good sense to channel my energy and put me in dancing school, because I was driving them crazy.
—Judith Jamison

Whatever our children's energy levels, activities can be a terrific way for them to explore their talents, broaden their interests, develop discipline, and make friends. Also, confidence gained on the soccer team, karate class, or dance lessons can spill over into social and academic areas.

Our schools just can't do it all, can't plumb and channel the potential in every child.

On this day, I will take five minutes to consider whether my child is getting enough physical activity.

PROGRESS

If there is no struggle, there is no progress.
—*Frederick Douglass*

The story of our people in America, and the story of our individual lives!

Some children never consider that a great report card can be theirs. If an A doesn't come easily, they start to think of themselves as B students. How unfortunate to lower their expectations for themselves at such a young age.

Just as we can be motivated by regularly visualizing ourselves succeeding at our dreams, our children can be inspired by visions of themselves winning the science fair prize, performing admirably at their recital, driving their soccer team to victory, and bringing home that report card overflowing with A's!

On this day I pledge to get my child off to a good start by underscoring the fact that, whatever she wants to achieve in life, it will take work and perseverance.

February 29

MONEY

Buyin' on credit is robbin' next year's crop.
—*African-American proverb*

Money woes can drain our spirit, souring our relations with our spouse *and* children.

No matter how bad things are right now, we can resolve that, barring unforeseen and unavoidable emergencies, they will get no worse. We might be able to find a higher-paying job or uncover opportunities for making extra cash. Let's not overlook or underestimate our talents. We might also tighten our budget, buy on sale, do without some indulgences, and enforce savings through automatic payroll deductions. If our affairs are more complicated, professional advice could be helpful. Let's assume a positive, committed and aggressive attitude as we square up against potentially ruinous spending habits.

On this day, I will take time to review my financial situation and make a list of things I might do to improve it.

LEGACY

*My grandmother and her third daughter, my
mother, put on maids' uniforms and cooked and
sewed and served a family that employed my
grandmother until she was nearly 80. I owe these
women everything. They taught me hope and
kindness and how to say thank you.*
—Patricia Raybon

How do we say "thank you"? Our words of appreciation
are important. Our mothers and aunts and grandmoth-
ers—our fathers and grandfathers, too—deserve to be
lauded for their diligence and sacrifice. Yet words alone
do not convey real gratitude. What is "thanks, Mom" if
we do not follow it up with our own effort? We must
teach our children that the positive attitude that fueled
our forebears' hard work must fuel ours.

*On this day, I will take five minutes to say to my child that
we honor the struggles of our forebears when we pursue our
dreams with zeal and determination.*

March 2

CULTURAL PURITY

*I am a man concerned with truth, not flattery, who
shares a dual culture that is unwilling to deny the
Harlem where I grew up or the Harlem of the Dutch
masters that contributed its element to my
understanding of art.*
—Romare Bearden

We are African Americans, yes, but first and foremost,
human beings. Why should we deny the wealth of human culture, whether emanating from Africa, Asia, Eu-
rope, or any spot on the globe?

Let's not worry about exposing our children to all
that is out there. Introducing them to the French Im-
pressionists does not imply we are negating our own heritage. It may be that they are inspired and excited by
Toni Morrison and James Joyce, too. Remember, Pi-
casso was influenced by African art and successfully
adapted it for his own purposes. We need not be reluctant to do the same.

*On this day, I will take five minutes to talk to my child about
the wealth of human culture around him and make sure he
knows that he is heir to all of it.*

SELF-DETERMINATION

*Remember, I wasn't supposed to last. I wasn't
supposed to be here ten years later, because I was
just supposed to be a flash in the pan.*
—Whoopi Goldberg

Remember, too, people will always make judgments
about us. They'll want to limit our rise or our staying
power. Often they do this in silence. But we will get the
idea, if we are alert. We will know if they do not intend
to promote us or even listen to us. When we know our
strengths and have nurtured a solid belief in ourselves,
we will find ways to deal with the limitations others will
try to impose upon us.

*On this day, I will take five minutes to talk to my child about
the importance of not being daunted
by others' opinions, which have no bearing
on our talent or our drive.*

EXCELLENCE

Our young brothers need to know how to live in both worlds.
— *Alvin F. Poussaint*

Sisters, too. We do our youth a disservice if we allow them to live by the notion that using proper grammar and making good grades are somehow "white" behavior. If we do not prepare our children to function in the business world, we are limiting their options and handicapping their potential progress. We must get across to our children that education is a part of *our* heritage, and that to brand it otherwise is to sell out our own African-American people.

On this day, I will take five minutes to talk with my child about black achievement. Then I will encourage him to let our talk inspire him in his work or studies throughout the day.

March 5

MANNERS

*We can all get very busy in life and forget to do the
basic "niceties" that we were taught. We forget
basic manners like calling, writing, touching, coming
to visit Mom and Dad.*
                                                —*Pearl Bailey*

Perhaps a few of us might rank a talk on manners as
pretty far down on our communal and personal agenda.
Yet courteousness and good manners have long been
part of our African-American tradition, tying in with
our feelings of personal dignity, the respect we are owed,
and the civility we have had to demand.

It's important to keep this tradition strong, because it
is both affirmative and uplifting. Let us start first in the
home, with our families, and then extend our consideration to others, especially to those in our African-
American community. How we talk to each other can
either enhance quality of life or detract from it.

*On this day, I will take five minutes to talk to my children
about manners, their place in our family, and in African-
American culture.*

SELF-IMAGE

Each of us, from childhood, weaves his own intricate web of self-images. These images form the beliefs born in response to every thought and experience, every humiliation and triumph, every defeat and victory.

—Dennis Kimbro

What tremendous influence we have upon our children's lives! Alert and attentive, we can monitor our child's experiences and thinking processes and help to shape a positive self-image.

We can teach our child that his humiliations and defeats are not due to any innate defect, but to specific behavior that can, in fact, be altered. We can celebrate the victories that underscore how good results come from effort and diligence.

Our sensitive guidance can make all the difference.

On this day I will take five minutes to think about the teaching approach that works best with my child and strive to keep her motivated and confident of success.

HELP

A wise parent knows when to look for help.
—Overheard on a New York City bus

There are times as parents that we're simply baffled. Perhaps our child is acting out at school, or not trying as hard in her schoolwork as she used to. Our attempts to reason and discipline seem to have no effect. We can't simply shrug our shoulders and give up; our child's future is at stake.

Let's commit to look for help wherever we can find it—at the principal's office, in a parent-teacher conference, in age-appropriate child-rearing books. There are people who have expertise that we don't; they may furnish clues to our child's behavior we hadn't considered and have suggestions and strategies for dealing with it. It is no slight on our abilities as parents if we have to look for help; on the contrary, it bespeaks the greatest devotion to our child and sends a message of commitment and faith from which our child will prosper.

On this day, I will take five minutes to consider whether I am stumped by any of my child's behavior. If so, I pledge to seek help in handling the situation.

FATHERHOOD

*A man ought to be concerned about where his
children go to school. He ought to be concerned
about whether they get the right things to eat and
wear, and whether they're going to church, and
about anything else that is happening to them.*
—Mary Frances Berry

What more needs to be said?

Our African-American fathers need to be men of
action. They need to be *involved,* on a daily basis—to
check homework, help with the science project, play ball
at the park, offer a hug or a pep talk.

We must guide our daughters to be selective when
choosing a mate; a man who does not respect her will
not respect their children. And we can teach our sons
that to be a black man is to be responsible, and to be a
black father is a positive, powerful experience.

*On this day, I will take five minutes to talk
with my child about men he admires and ask
why he admires them.*

DIRECTION

*I knew what I wanted to do with my life, and it was
show business to its fullest potential.*
—*Eddie Murphy*

As a youngster, Eddie Murphy had a vision. He knew he
would be a star, and he had the will, the confidence, and
the talent to make his dream reality.

It might make us feel uneasy if our own child's
dreams are less clear. How can we help bring things into
focus so she isn't a victim of indecision and poor planning? Let's give her the time to figure out what it is that
excites her, that gives her pleasure and a sense of fulfillment. Does she see herself as a top pastry chef, a child
psychologist, an advertising mogul? With commitment
and hard work she must know she can realize her vision
and reach her fullest potential.

*On this day, I will take five minutes to think about or talk to
my child about her future.*

CONTENTMENT

Blessed are those who can please themselves.
—*Zulu proverb*

Funny how no one ever teaches you how to find contentment. Some of us manage it, however, by teaching ourselves. When we are attuned to what gives us pleasure and fulfillment, we gain a healthy sense of independence and self-knowledge.

Our children are even more susceptible to outside influences, some of which can be injurious to their development. We can help them to withstand peer pressure by encouraging them to tap into interests and activities that make life meaningful for them. When our children learn to please themselves in wholesome ways, they're less likely to resort to self-destructive pastimes— or feel the need to please everyone else.

On this day, I will take five minutes to work with my child on something that grabs him. It might be karate or guitar, poetry or crafts, skating, dance, or reading.

PRIORITIES

*Your father didn't sacrifice to send you to that
school so you could join a social club. If those white
boys start interfering with your education, then you
can get back to me.*
                                        —*"Aunt" Bennie*

Scene: the late 1960s. I was attending Bancroft Junior
High in Los Angeles, a school that enjoyed a great rep-
utation. I had complained that a particular group of
boys seemed to be ostracizing me socially. I mentioned
this to my aunt, and that is when she made her state-
ment.

Obviously, we all want to be liked, and it's true
that social contacts lead to job and financial opportunities. But my aunt's point was that if I focused on the
primary reason I was there and performed well in that
capacity, good things would follow, regardless of those
boys.

*On this day, I will talk to my child about the importance of
focus. I will emphasize that if you know what you are looking
for from a given situation, you will have the strength to
weather storms large and small.*

March 12

PRODUCTIVITY

*To this day I'm an early riser. That comes from
Dad always saying, "Off and on," meaning: "Off
your ass and on the deck." He didn't like us lying
around; we had to be productive.*
—Reggie Jackson

Half the trick in life is learning how to use our time well.
We want to discourage lazy habits while, at the same
time, allowing for the "downtime" we all need to dream,
think, and grow. And with all that, we need to take our
child's temperament into consideration.

A little common sense can guide us. If our child
has a busy schedule, is applying himself at school and
showing good results, has practiced his piano, gotten
ample exercise, and kept his room in reasonable condition, a late Saturday wake-up call or a few hours "hang-
ing out" might be in order to refresh his spirit and
energy. On the other hand, daily TV or video-game
binges followed by "sleeping in" should signal us to do
something—fast.

*On this day, I will take five minutes to consider
whether my child is using his time in a productive,
balanced manner.*

APPROPRIATENESS

I have found thoughts and words to be the foundation for success and failure in life. I'm teaching my kids when to whisper and when to shout.

—*Diana Ross*

As adults we have by now learned that there are indeed times to whisper and times to shout. Shouting all the time is not effective; people cease to hear you after a while. So, too, there are times to speak up so as to be heard and not ignored.

Just as our children must learn when to adjust the volume, they must also know that there are times to say nothing—to do more research, think things over, sleep on it. When they are ready, they can then put their thoughts into the kind of words that will be compelling, persuasive, and effective.

On this day, I will take five minutes to talk to my child about how different situations call for different kinds of verbal persuasion: sometimes soft, sometimes aggressive, sometimes emotional, sometimes intellectual.

CUSTODIANSHIP

For too long we have been defined, examined, analyzed, and judged by others. Others, mainly whites, have decided what aspects of our past should be remembered. In jazz, we don't control the film footage of our greatest musicians; in sports, we don't control film footage of our greatest athletes. We don't even control much of our folklore, because it was collected by others, and they control the copyright.

We don't need to blame or try to stop whites, for their records are in many ways invaluable. But we must, with renewed vigor, continue, in the tradition of the filmmaker Oscar Michaux, the folklorist Zora Neale Hurston, and the historian G. Carter Woodson, to bear witness and document our own people's lives.

On this day, I will encourage my child to be a custodian of our people, to look at our art, listen to our music, witness our struggles, and document his impressions, even if in a diary.

March 15

EXPLORATION

I patterned myself from classy ladies. I take as much from them as I can, but I take it naturally, because I'm not going to be phony about it.
—Tina Turner

We are our own inventions, and we invent ourselves by becoming aware of the range of possibilities out there and deciding what appeals to us, what image we want to project, and how we want to live our lives.

We may fear looking or acting "phony," but the choices we make are manifestations of our inner desires and needs. We are free to change and free to pick and choose the style that most suits us now. Observing us, our children learn that they need not conform to trends that do not suit them. They, too, must be allowed the freedom to stretch themselves to see what excites their passion, what motivates and inspires them. Perhaps our child can teach *us* something new.

On this day, I will take five minutes to consider whether I make snide remarks that may dampen my child's enthusiasm or curb her exploration. If so, I pledge to stop.

CREDENTIALS

*Ah, I sometimes think, to be able to hit them over
the head with my résumé.*
—Stephen L. Carter

As Carter points out: "Social psychologists report that
even white people who indulge in a great deal of stereo-
typing will alter their opinions of black people who possess identifiable status attainments, such as advanced
degrees."

It's not that we want our children to fret over getting white people to like them. In fact, the same mech-
anism is in play with black people. Life is a succession of
judgment calls, and credentials give the judge a reason
to vote in your favor, black or white. Picking up credentials in your chosen field will facilitate attaining your
goals in your profession; performance will keep you
there.

*On this day, I will take five minutes to talk with my child
about what he wants to accomplish in life, then will consider
credentials—contests he can enter, awards he might win—
that would advance him toward his goal.*

OPTIMISM

*Everyone, regardless of how naturally optimistic he
or she is, has to work at remaining positive.*
—Lenda Murray

There are just some folks who seem eternally positive.
No matter what ill fortune befalls them, they manage to
keep the faith.

What is the source of their optimism—and how
can *we* tap into it? It's not a matter of magic or mystery.
There are very likely moments of doubt, worry, or gloom
with which even the most relentlessly optimistic must
cope. But if we can make it a *habit* to seek out sustenance or motivation in ways that work for us personally—whether through prayer, by reaching into
ourselves, or by looking at or listening to whatever feeds
us inspiration—we can learn to find strength when we
need it.

*On this day, I will take five minutes to talk to my child about
ways to identify the things that make her feel better, so that
she might not linger in negativity, but work her way out of it.*

March 18

SELF-WORTH

No one can leave a permanent mark on the world till he learns to be true to himself.
—Paul Robeson

It's possible that, as adults, we're *still* fighting to be true to ourselves. So how do we help our children with this one? Let's ask: Have I encouraged them from an early age to be critical thinkers? Enabling them to weed out inappropriate choices can help them to stand up to outside pressures that can be detrimental. Have we instructed them in determining their own priorities, forming their own standards, respecting their own feelings and conclusions? Do we give them opportunities to make decisions and take stands? Those things take practice, and we have to allow them their occasional regrettable ideas and sloppy judgment without convincing them that they are somehow lacking or inept. Our personal example can do a lot to guide them, even when they appear cantankerously critical or uninterested.

On this day, I will take five minutes to list five things I can do to be a better parent.

COMMUNICATION

*I am most passionate in my relationship with
mama. It is with her that I feel loved and sometimes
accepted. She is the one person who looks into my
heart, sees its needs, and tries to satisfy them.*
—bell hooks

There will be times we lose patience with our children,
times either they will retreat sullenly into their rooms or
that *we* will cut them off.

Let there also be times we look into their hearts,
times we come out of ourselves to empathize with them,
times of communion that reinforce the bond between
us. It is out of these times that our child will know the
love and acceptance that they will carry with them
through life.

*On this day, I will take five minutes to consider
whether I am listening carefully enough to
my child and expressing the love I feel for her.
If not, I pledge to do so.*

COMPETITION

*In and out of school, I have always been motivated
by a spirit of competition, particularly when pitted
against white people.*
—Ralph Bunche

Whatever works. It's certainly better to be motivated to
compete than to be paralyzed by anger or envy.

In 1950 Ralph Bunche, member of the United
Nations Secretariat, won the Nobel Peace Prize for negotiating an armistice agreement that ended the first
Arab-Israeli war. Did his considerable accomplishment
have anything to do with, as he puts it, "Nana's constant admonition to let them, especially white folks,
know that you can do anything they can do"? We don't
need to use *whites* as a measure of our success. *Any* op-
ponent will do. Many successful people are motivated by
competition. Why not make it work for us?

*On this day, I will take five minutes to talk to my child about
competition and how it can challenge him to excel in any
given endeavor.*

LABELING

Everybody loves a fool, but nobody wants him for
a son.
                                        —*Malinke proverb*

What do we see when we look at our child? A fool, or someone with a gift for making people laugh? A nerd, or a decent, intellectually gifted person?

What may seem a disadvantage in youth may account for success in adulthood. The awkwardness will fade, the ragged edges will be smoothed, and our child will learn to express all aspects of his personality in order to integrate himself with ease into the social flow.

On this day, I will take five minutes to think of what might
seem a disadvantageous trait in my child, and imagine how
it might fade or transform into
a positive trait in the future.

COMFORT

Our strength is that we are not comfortable any place; therefore, we're comfortable every place. We can go any place on earth and find a way to be comfortable.
—*Nikki Giovanni*

We cannot permit our discomfort to keep us from functioning as parents, or as individuals. If, for example, our local school system seems largely dominated by whites, we cannot let that prevent us from getting involved, going to meetings, trying to head the PTA. In fact, if we are skeptical or pessimistic about "the system," then we should be doubly sure to participate. Nor is it appropriate for us to steer our children away from talents or interests we regard as "white" activities for the sole purpose of sparing them discomfort.

On this day, I will take time to list five ways I can provide a warmer, more secure home environment, so that my child will be better equipped to go where her dreams and ambitions take her, to be comfortable in her skin, and truly free of others' limited and faulty perceptions.

RESPONSIBILITY

*At first color doesn't mean very much to little
children, black or white. Only as they grow older and
absorb poisons from adults does color begin to blind
them.*

—Roy Wilkins

There's not a great deal we can do about the poison
white children receive, but we *can* try to detox our own
child's environment. As we embrace our history and
culture, and speak of our people in positive terms, we
can enforce the point that, through our will and effort,
we can achieve anything we set our minds to achieving.

*On this day, I will take five minutes to discuss with my child
an item relating to black pride—kente cloth, for instance, or a
family photograph—and suggest
that he let that object inspire him to excellence
throughout the day.*

March 24

EFFORT

*It is true that in crucial situations, I have lost
matches. But I knew I was giving 110 percent.*
—Zina Garrison

When it comes down to that crucial moment, everything counts. Our training regimen, the amount of
sleep we had the night before, our mental/emotional
state. If one area is lacking or neglected, our performance can suffer. But if we are in peak condition, giving 110 percent and still we "lose," we have nothing to
chastise ourselves for. We might assess the situation,
determine what factors contributed to our defeat, and
ponder how we might better address them.

*On this day, I will take five minutes to talk with my child
about defeats, emphasizing that the only reason to be
ashamed of them is if we don't analyze them and use them to
make a stronger showing the next time.*

RELIGION

You know what religion is? You got ta live religion.
You got ta do religion. You got ta live Right.
—Mance Lipscomb

Yes, religion is more than our particular denomination, more than the frequency with which we attend church or a mosque, more than how much we put into the collection basket. Religion is how we treat each other. It is fairness, decency, generosity, kindness, and caring. It comes from inside and is manifested in our everyday acts and interactions.

We may be troubled if our child starts to question our beliefs or becomes cynical. But let us look further into his heart and soul before we castigate his spiritual commitment. His prayers may sound different than ours, but they come from the same place.

On this day, I pledge to do my religion so that my child will view it as a positive alternative to the soulless ways that are out there.

DAUGHTERS

The sad truth is that too many girls' spirits, self-esteem, and self-image are still being warped, their needs ignored, their voices stilled.
—Marcia Ann Gillespie

Marcia Ann Gillespie makes it plain: Too many of our girls are dancing to music calling them bitches, having sex because they want affection, having babies to give themselves status, and downplaying their intelligence in general. What on earth has gone wrong?

When a child is not respected, she has a hard time learning how to respect herself. When encouragement is lacking, she can lose the motivation to develop her mind and talents. When no one takes an interest in her "present," is it likely she'll take much of an interest in her future?

On this day, if I have a daughter, I will tell her that she should settle for nothing less than respect. If I have a son, I will make sure to tell him that he should have respect for members of the opposite sex.

MOTIVATION

*You cannot teach what you don't know. You cannot
give energy if you're not on fire on the inside.*
—Jesse Jackson

This doesn't mean *we* have to be rocket scientists before
our child can become one. It means that we do our jobs
with a purpose in mind—to create opportunities for our
child and to light the fire that will enable our child to
take off.

If our own fire inside sometimes seems on the
verge of being extinguished, we can use the hopes we
have for our children to help fan the flames.

*On this day, I will remember that even the most tedious
tasks can be made more bearable by realizing that seeing me
shouldering responsibility will help my children learn what it
takes to be successful in the world.*

POSITIVE ATTITUDE

African-Americans can not only create music, but control it as well.
                                        —*Sylvia Rhone*

Time and again, African Americans have ignored others' notions of what we are "incapable" of doing and succeeded in a big way. We are surgeons, scientists, lawyers, scholars, bank presidents, stockbrokers, and CEOs. Our children need to know this.

On this day, I will pledge to encourage my child's interests and talents and expose him to all he can do and be. I will do my best to foster a positive attitude, a desire to excel, a commitment to proper work/study habits, and the ability to persevere despite obstacles and setbacks.

March 29

DIVERSITY

Whence all this passion toward conformity
anyway?—diversity is the word.
—Ralph Ellison

Diversity is our strength. It does us no good to separate
the conservatives from the liberals, the integrationists
from the separatists, the bankers from the griots. Why
not pool our wealth of ideas, talents, and resources,
and from them build up our community so that all will
prosper.

On this day, I will take five minutes to remind my child that,
although as African Americans we may be playing different
positions in the great game of life, the vast majority of us
ultimately have the same goals: true financial empowerment,
true political empowerment, and real education and freedom.
And what kind of team would it be anyway, if everyone
played one position?

March 30

SANCTUARY

Soon after the birth of my second child, I found the roles of wife, housekeeper, daughter, sister and mother overwhelming. I decided I had to create a space for myself. A place where I could go to gain repose, to tend to myself, to sort out my thoughts, lay my burdens down and commune with God.
—Sarah Boyd

Sarah Boyd re-created her bedroom to suit her fantasies and needs. Even if we lack the wherewithal to turn an entire room into the sanctuary we'd like, let's be creative. Perhaps there's a corner by a sunny window that would be just right for a cozy chair covered with Grandma's quilt, with a little stand or table nearby to hold a flowering plant, a scented pillar candle, and a pretty mug for our tea. We'll be happy we've made the effort.

On this day, I will make a list of things I can do to create a sanctuary for myself.

LAUGHTER

As my mother had done for me, I told my son jokes and encouraged him to laugh at himself. The Black child must learn early to allow laughter to fill his mouth or the million small cruelties he encounters will congeal and clog his throat.
—Maya Angelou

Children love to laugh. For most, it comes quite naturally. And they love to see *us* laugh, too. Yet while we are raising them to be capable, productive individuals, we may sometimes get lost in the seriousness of our mission.

African Americans have long tapped into our senses of humor in order to get through some of our bad days with our spirits intact. Picking out the absurdities in life and being able to laugh at them relieves stress, maintains sanity, and simply feels good. Laughing at our children's jokes validates their self-esteem and cements the bond between us. These moments of lightness make for memories our children will treasure through their adult lives.

On this day, I will take five minutes with my child to laugh at something funny or incongruous in the world.

FAMILY CONVERSATION

Conversation is food for the ear.
—Trinidadian proverb

How are our family conversations these days? Not the hasty exchanges we have to determine the whereabouts of socks or the time of dinner, but the occasions when we really listen to one another, respond to, challenge, and enlighten each other.

We can start when our children first learn to talk, encouraging them to express themselves and share their observations of the world. Later on, our dinner-table topics might touch on politics, sports, books, school and community news, popular culture—anything that appeals to us. Through constant "quality talk," our children will gain confidence in their ability to articulate themselves and to think critically—valuable skills that will aid them throughout life. Let's remember not to be too harsh or judgmental with our children; they have to feel home is a safe place to make themselves heard.

On this day, I will take time to talk to my child about something that is important to her.

CONTRADICTIONS

*I'm moved by the contraries, by opposites, the
strength that was my mother's eyes, the beauty of
my father's hands.*
—Judith Jamison

We, too, can be similarly moved—by the tenderness of
our son's embrace at bedtime, by the sureness with
which our daughter attacks a math problem or a soccer
ball.

Let's be accepting and appreciative of all aspects
of our child's personality, and avoid trying to edit out
attributes *we* deem unmasculine or unfeminine. It is
this very precious mix of qualities that makes our child
unique and lovable.

*On this day, I will take time to tell my child about five things
I like about him.*

WHITE PEOPLE

I stopped thinking that all white folks were out to get me.
—Nathan McCall

First off, most white folks simply don't care about us one way or another, and many of those who *are* negatively disposed toward us are probably inclined to dismiss or mistreat *any* group of people they judge to be powerless.

Let's stop worrying about white people; let's get some power! For our children, acquiring power translates into good grades, academic awards, involvement in school activities, and the development and recognition of special talents. While honors and awards are not an end in themselves, they provide our children with options for their lives and confidence in their abilities. Armed with these things, our children are less at the mercy of what white people think about them and more in control of their own destiny.

On this day, I will take five minutes to talk to my child about what she likes and dislikes in school, ways to make the subjects she dislikes more appetizing, and areas in which she needs to improve.

STRESS

On bad days like that I always make a mess of greens. Besides the curative properties, the ritual of fixing the greens—handling each green personally, folding leaf unto leaf, cutting them up, etc.—cools me out.
    —Vertamae Smart Grosvenor

These days we need an arsenal of ways to destress, things we can do to regain our spiritual balance that don't make us fat, drunk, or ashamed.

What works for us? Reading poetry, kneading bread dough, listening to Aretha, a walk through the park, or a long soak in the tub? Maybe we need to experiment.

Before we carp at our mates or lose it with our children, before we wolf down too many cookies or margueritas, let's take charge of our stress.

On this day, I will come up with a list of at least five ways I can seek relaxation and release of stress.

PARENTAL ROLE MODELS

*If you're lucky, you grow up in a house where you
can learn what kind of person you should be from
your parents. And on that count I was very lucky.*
—Michael Jordan

The standards to which we hold our children should be
no higher than the standards to which we hold ourselves. If we expect them to be industrious, then *we*
must be industrious. Ditto any adjective we would like
to be able to ascribe to them: fair-minded, considerate,
determined—you name it. Of course, our children will
have their own personalities and temperament, vulnerabilities and strengths. There are no guarantees that
they will mirror every good quality we possess, but as
they move into the world, they may come to value the
modes of behavior that are familiar to them. As parents
we can never underestimate the amount of influence we
have on our children. Let's make sure that the example
we provide them with is one we'd like to see them reflect.

*On this day, I will take five minutes to think about what
kind of role model I am for my child, and if I need
improvement, I pledge to do better.*

LIFE'S BATTLES

*I have a right to stay here. With all that my parents
and grandparents gave to Mississippi, I have a
right to stay here and fight for what they didn't get.*
—Fannie Lou Hamer

For all that our ancestors gave and didn't get, we have
not just the right, but the responsibility, to fight for our
piece of the American dream. Our individual "fights"
may appear small or insignificant, but cumulatively
they pose a brighter future for our people.

Our own fight begins with that American dream
inside our minds—the kind of life we envision for ourselves and our family. As with any fight, we must prepare ourselves well, sustain our morale through
dispiriting times, and refuse to surrender. Through us,
our children learn both strategy and the will to victory.

*On this day, I will take five minutes to consider whether I
am adequately preparing my child to handle life's battles and
storms.*

EMOTIONS

*Express positive emotions of love, happiness, and
self-confidence. Negative emotions are destructive;
positive emotions heal.*
—*John E. Copage*

Negative emotions sap our mind and body. They make
us snap at our children, pick fights with our mates, have
an "attitude" at work. When we are so full of negative
feelings, there's no room for positive ones to come in—
such as the love and affection of family and friends or
opportunities for improving our lives.

Acknowledging the positive we do will put us in a
better frame of mind and allow for more love, happiness,
and self-confidence to enter our lives.

*On this day, I will take time with my child to jot on separate
pieces of paper five things we have done that have given us
pleasure or gratification today—anything from a half-hour
walk at lunch to reading a story to cleaning out our closet.*

April 8

BLACK MEN AND BLACK WOMEN

*Whoever walked behind anyone to freedom? If we
can't go hand-in-hand I don't want to go.*
                                        —Hazel Scott

Hazel Scott said that twenty years ago. After two dec-
ades, black men and women are still fussing with each
other. Will our children find the same situation as they
reach adulthood?

We need to teach our children that, to achieve the
"unity" we all talk and sing about, we must show respect
for one another and work together. When our child
comes home with a sexist remark, let's not simply let it
go. We need to address his/her reasons for making the
comment and ask whether this kind of thinking is productive to our joint efforts to empower all African
Americans.

*On this day, I will pledge that, when talking to my children,
I will resist sexist blather and emphasize
the fact that black men and women are in
the same struggle and shouldn't siphon their energies
sniping at one another.*

OPPORTUNITY

Affirmative action begins at home.
—*Detroit barber*

As parents, we have to be driven to mine every opportunity that can benefit our children. No excuses. Whether we are short on time, energy, or money, there are always ways we can get what we want for our children. If we don't find them at first, we have to keep on looking. It might take a dozen phone calls, some cajoling, planning, or creative problem solving, but aren't our children worth it?

On this day, I will take five minutes to consider whether I am exhausting every opportunity to secure opportunities that will permit my child to stretch to his potential and get in touch with what life has to offer.

DEPRESSION

I just don't get really depressed that society hasn't lived up to its obligations, so depressed I would not keep challenging or keep trying to do whatever I could to open up some space for people to realize where we are and where we need to get to.
—Charlayne Hunter-Gault

Not one of us can afford to get so depressed that we become immobilized. Yes, we'll feel discouraged from time to time. Weary, too. In those moments, we need to locate those things in our lives that can give us the strength and motivation to rally our spirits and plunge ahead.

On this day I will take five minutes to do something that recharges my spirits—it might be reciting a prayer, looking at a photograph of my parents or grandparents, reading a book—or best of all, looking at my children.

April 11

PRAISE

I did not realize it then, but the phrase, "We are very proud of you," always with the emphasis on very, boosted me immeasurably through the years.
—*Jonah Martin Edelman*

Our sentiments of pride and praise must come not only after success, but after defeat and disappointment, too. It is, after all, not just their A's and home runs that make our children so precious to us.

Warm affirmations and expressions of love motivate our children to make their best effort. Let's time them well so that our child knows our love is not contingent on performance.

On this day, I will take five minutes to consider whether I express pride in my child only after she has succeeded in some specific task.

EXERCISE

*Fitness can be as easy as calling a friend and going
for a walk around the neighborhood. Even better,
take your husband and kids along and make fitness
a family affair.*
—Florence Griffith Joyner

Who says family fun and togetherness has to cost a lot
of money or require a lot of energy? Perhaps a weekend
walk, bike ride, swim, or basketball game can become a
family tradition. The local Y might also have a "family
night" that can get us moving and laughing instead of
fighting over which TV show to watch.

*On this day, I will suggest to my family that we engage in
some sort of physical exercise together. And if
they are preoccupied or uninterested, I will do it alone
or with a friend.*

April 13

INDIVIDUAL RESPONSIBILITY

*Sometimes the runt pig beats the whole litter
growing.*
—African-American proverb

No doubt about it, we of African descent are having a
difficult time worldwide. Famine, revolution, AIDS,
rampant crime, petty dictators, and political oppression
seem sometimes as if they will tear our people asunder.
But we mustn't despair. We must remember the principles that made the African empires of Mali, Ghana,
and Songhai grand; the dedication of our freedom
movements; the integrity of our greatest individuals.
But our return to greatness won't happen with a five-
point plan of a Great Black Leader, nor with the stroke
of a pen passing more legislation. It will happen only if
each of us takes responsibility for being the strongest
link possible between future generations and the past.

*On this day, I will ask myself, "How strong a link between
our past and our promise am I? And am I preparing my
child to be the strongest link he can be?"*

April 14

SELF-CONFIDENCE

*Do I believe I'm blessed? Of course I do! In the first
place, my mother told me so, many, many times,
and when she did it was always quietly, confidently.*
—*Duke Ellington*

Duke Ellington was indeed blessed—with both enormous talent and a loving, supportive mother.

How wonderful for a child to approach the world
feeling blessed! Our young one needn't have incredible
riches at his disposal or talents befitting a prodigy. But
each child does have an array of gifts, interests, and
skills that make him or her special, plus time to develop
those. With our love, help, and encouragement, our
child can realize his full potential—and what greater
blessing than that?

*On this day, I will compliment my child
on at least one thing.*

TEMPERAMENT

*I was an odd child; I was extremely introverted, very
quiet. And my mother would allow that because she
was also an introvert; we were kindred spirits.*
—Gloria Naylor

What happens when we are not "kindred spirits"? The
things our child says and does may baffle or frustrate us.
Perhaps we've tried to exhort her to "be more like her
brother" or "less like her father." It can be vastly more
frustrating for our child to be told, in effect, that her
true nature is unacceptable to us.

Often that quality of hers that gives us pause can
be redefined in more positive terms. For example, boss-
iness can be seen as displaying leadership qualities.

*On this day I will take five minutes to talk
with my child and praise her for at least five things
that make her unique.*

April 16

FAILURE

I don't have anything to fear, you know? I'm 24. I don't expect to make a hit every time.
—*John Singleton*

Director John Singleton knows that whether we're 14, 24, or 64, if we curb our dreams because we're afraid to risk failure, we're not going to give ourselves room to stretch or explore our talents.

Let's start our child off with a healthy attitude. There will be sports losses, wrong answers in class, social embarrassments, and disappointing test scores. These occasions, temporarily painful as they may be, are learning experiences. Rather than chastise our child for her defeat, let's help her to discover what she needs to do differently for better results next time.

On this day, I will take five minutes to remember that if my child does poorly in a given circumstance, it is not the end of the world. The most important question is: Did he give it his all? And the next day we can analyze how to improve future performances.

April 17

STORIES

When I was young, stories were a big thing in our house. Sometimes the stories came from books, but generally the stories centered around my parents' experiences as young children. These stories allowed me to build powerful images of myself as a young girl and as a woman.

—Julia A. Boyd

Stories are a wonderful way to connect with our children. They don't have to entail high adventure, and we don't have to be master storytellers, either. The importance is in the sharing and in the breaking down of barriers between us. When it's a personal story from our youth, our child is exposed to another part of us, one with which they can identify.

Hearing about our family experiences helps our child to feel connected to something bigger than himself and gives him a vital sense of tradition and communion.

On this day, I will share a story about myself with my child.

April 18

DISAGREEMENT

Too much agreement kills a chat.
—Eldridge Cleaver

But wouldn't it be nice if, some days, there were just a wee bit more agreement and a little less dissension around the house?

Not infrequently, the decibel level goes up when our children are in dispute about something or other, and it can surely get on our nerves. But before we rush in to shush them, let's give them another moment to resolve things on their own. Sometimes it works, and it can help them to learn a thing or two about empathy and cooperation.

A dinner-table debate does not have to disrupt the harmony of the household if it is carried on in a reasonable manner—no name-calling, abusiveness, or stomping off in tears. It does a child good to be able to speak up for herself, to refuse to swallow someone else's "logic," and learn how to defend and support her position.

On this day, I will encourage my child to speak her mind in a well-reasoned, rational manner.

INITIATIVE

If I have a philosophy of life, it's about making your own way. Going out and getting it done. Not expecting it to be done for you.
—*Janet Jackson*

It doesn't hurt to have had the kind of leg up in life that Janet Jackson had—a famous show-business family with contacts and clout. But even Janet Jackson had to produce, to go out on her own, to mine and develop her talents as we must mine and develop ours. Our children must know: No one presents us with a fulfilling career on a silver platter, but we can serve ourselves.

On this day, I will talk to my child about the importance of hard work, persistence, and resourcefulness in attaining one's goals, and that this diligence will make our achievement that much more special.

April 20

RISK

*I was drawn to dangerous things. Ever since I can
remember I have enjoyed being scared a little bit.*
—Sidney Poitier

We're not talking about foolish or unwholesome "danger" here, but the kind of risk taking that comes with accepting challenges and stretching beyond what feels comfortable and familiar.

Does our child shy away from challenges for fear of putting himself on the line and perhaps failing? Or is he worried that his friends will mock his ambition? If he succumbs to either fear, he will never reach his potential. But our warm congratulations and the pleasure success affords will show our child it's okay to be a little scared—because he can rise above it in triumph.

*On this day, I will pledge to help my child overcome his fears.
For an older child, I will encourage him to visualize success.
For a younger child, I will begin getting him in the habit of
taking on new things—a speaking part in the school play or
an art class—as simple ways for him to gain confidence in
meeting new challenges.*

PARENTHOOD

I had to become a mother before I realized what a wonderful place in the scheme of things the creator has given woman.
—Ida B. Wells

Of course, that's not always easy to keep in mind, especially when "woman" is trying to put together a meal, help with the homework, entertain a toddler, and rotate loads of laundry, all before paying bills and making the PTA meeting. In *that* scheme of things, parenthood might start to lose a little of its luster. What we might need to do in the midst of our difficult moments is to think back to the funny joke our son made up, or consider the way our daughter is working so hard on her science project, or recall the attention our eldest paid to our youngest when we were too busy. Little things, but they can help put things into perspective.

On this day I will take five minutes to remember the joy my child has given me over the years.

April 22

PREPARATION

*A toga that one drapes while running also comes
untied while one is running.*
—*Ethiopian proverb*

Without adequate preparation, we cannot expect good results. This goes across the board—schoolwork, sports, careers, fixing dinner. We cannot count on luck to save us.

Nor can we expect our children to compete if we have not trained them for competition. Even a strong will to win can be frustrated if it meets with defeat time and again because of sloppy training. (Read: if we study, practice, rehearse, make lists, and take stock of what we have and what we need victory is ours.) Good habits can make or break their chances.

When we send our children out to participate in the race of life, let's make sure we have prepared them mentally, physically, spiritually.

*On this day, I will take five minutes to consider whether I
am adequately training my child for the world. If not, I
pledge to start doing so.*

LEARNING

Something dawned on me, like a big light bulb over my noggin. I suddenly understood that I didn't know a hell of a lot about anything. What it was that seemed to move me then was that learning was important.

—*Amiri Baraka*

Amiri Baraka resolved, at that moment, to learn something new every day, simply for the pleasure of learning.

While we are trying to coax the best out of our children, it's important to point out the enjoyment and gratification to be derived from their studies. There are ways to make things more interesting, such as visiting a museum exhibit, planetarium, or science center that might augment current subject matter.

Let's not neglect our teachers, too, who may have wonderful suggestions to pique the interest of our children.

On this day, I will find something of beauty and joy in the world and share it with my child.

POSITIVE INFLUENCES

*I'll be damned if I want most folks out there to do
unto me what they do unto themselves. There are a
whole lot of unevolved, self-destructive wretches out
there walking around on the loose.*
—Toni Cade Bambara

Yes, and some are friends and family. They may want to
discourage us because they have talked themselves out
of their dreams. They may tempt us with overindul-
gence because *they* overindulge. They might simply cast
a pall over our days with their gloomy outlook on life.

If there are people we absolutely cannot cut out of
our lives, then we will have to be strong. We must let
them know that their negativity brings us down and that
we cannot tolerate their foul moods. It could happen
that our good habits and positive energy will make con-
verts out of them, but it is really not our job to save
them.

*On this day, I pledge to keep a watchful eye on my child's
friends, and gently to encourage her to focus on those who
seem positive and focused.*

April 25

LUCK

*There're a lot of chance encounters in life. To come
from where I come from and go to college when I was
bound for the shipyards, to graduate from the
University of Chicago, that's a lot of serendipity
and chance.*
                                                    —Brent Staples

Unquestionably, luck plays a part in our lives. It's bo-
gus, however, to believe that others get all the good luck
and *we* get all the bad.

Author and *New York Times* editorial board member Brent Staples was indeed bound for the shipyards
when a chance encounter with a college professor gifted
him with the phone number for a college admissions director. Staples could have tossed the number, convinced
of his own meager luck, but, no, he made the phone call
that was a first step in changing the direction of his life.

Let's teach our children to be alert when "luck"
comes their way.

*On this day, I will take five minutes to talk to
my child about luck—that half of it is recognizing it
when it appears.*

April 26

SCHOOLING/TEACHERS

*I had a lot of people tell me I couldn't write. In fact,
very few of my teachers encouraged me to believe
that I could write.*
—Margaret Walker

For whatever reasons—conscious or unconscious bigotry, inattention, or simple lack of time, energy, or vision—our children's teachers do not always give them the kind of encouragement they deserve. What can *we* do?

We can first search out all the wonderful and caring teachers who will help to motivate our child. We can talk to other parents and submit a request to the principal before class assignments are made. School policy differs. Some principals do not welcome specific teacher requests but are open to letters from parents describing their child's personality/temperament/strengths and will try to pair them with a teacher who will best suit the child's needs.

On this day, I pledge to stay on top of what is happening in my child's classroom—through both frequent conversation with our child and regular chats with the teacher.

April 27

ENCOURAGEMENT

*My dad's probably the sole reason I'm playing
tennis, in that it was his love of the game that kept
us from drifting away from it. He definitely pushed
us along, and I know I needed that.*
—Mali Vai Washington

It's not always the easiest thing to know what our children need, or how far to push them. What spurs one
child on might cause resentment in another. We just
have to gauge it as best we can. Perhaps the teacher or
instructor has some worthwhile input—let's ask. We
might also try a schedule change, lightening up a bit but
not pulling out totally. Our child might also benefit by
having a partner, someone her age whose enthusiasm
and participation would bolster her own. Then, again, if
we were hoping for a star basketball forward but our
child is set on pouring his energies into the student
council or the debate team, we must recognize these
other interests as areas for our child to excel in in a way
that is meaningful to him.

*On this day, I will take five minutes to think about the
specific needs of my child and how best to cater to them.*

CREATIVITY

Cease to be a drudge, seek to be an artist.
—Mary McLeod Bethune

There is joy in completing our simplest tasks with flair and creativity. Most of us won't become artists in the literal sense of the word, but we can apply the same focus and intensity to whatever we do. It makes the job itself more interesting and the outcome more gratifying.

It helps to learn this early, so let's encourage our children to give their all to their schoolwork. A first grader assigned to draw a picture for homework will have a lot more fun with it when guided to use his imagination, be creative with his technique, and inject some fantasy or humor into it. Suddenly homework turns into a playful endeavor, a source of pride and not just drudge work. This same attitude can carry our child through years of assignments and term papers, challenging him to do his best and rewarding him with pleasure in learning.

On this day, I will take five minutes to work with my child on an assignment and we will look for ways to make it better by employing creativity and artfulness.

ENVIRONMENTALISM

My wish is that we would allow this planet to be the beautiful oasis that she is, and allow ourselves to live more in the peace that she generates.
—Ronald E. McNair

A filthy environment is degrading to us, to our children, too. It shows lack of respect, lack of vision, hopelessness.

Let's begin in our homes to do what we can to beautify our world. Recycling cans, bottles, and newspapers is a fine place to start. Making that effort gives us confidence in our ability to make a difference on a global scale.

Let's raise children who care about the rain forests and who wouldn't think of dropping gum wrappers on the street—whether it's in front of our home or a thousand miles away. This world belongs to *all* of us, so let's show pride of ownership.

On this day, when with my child, I pledge to pick up at least one piece of trash off the ground and throw it in the nearby trash can. And I pledge to discuss an environmental issue elsewhere in the world and a concrete way we can take action together to help alleviate it.

April 30

INVOLVEMENT

*The white kids never hesitated to hold up their
hands in response to a teacher's question; even
when they were wrong they were wrong aggressively.*
—Maya Angelou

Our children need to be able to compete in this world. To do that, they must be able to put up their hands and act like they know what they're talking about. Yes, ideally it's best if they've got the right answer, but even the wrong answer will bring them to the teacher's attention. If they're wrong, they can recover from that and move on.

Getting in the game is the idea. Whether in school or in life, our children must be encouraged to participate with boldness and confidence.

*On this day, I will take five minutes to talk to my child about
the importance of speaking up in class and
in life. For, as the lottery slogan goes—you got
to be in it to win it.*

May 1

BAD BEHAVIOR

*People do not wish to be worse, they really wish to
become better, but they often do not know how.*
—James Baldwin

Warning: Our children, too, will make mistakes, be led
astray, act foolishly, stubbornly, in a perplexing manner. Let's bear this in mind the next time we find ourselves shaking our heads over some new mischief our
child has perpetrated. Let's not merely react with rage
and punishment.

*On this day, if my child acts up, I will count to ten and try
to handle the situation firmly, but calmly, with an aim
toward helping him make better decisions in the future. And
when he does something good, I will be sure to praise him
with enthusiasm.*

May 2

COMPLACENCY

Big blanket make man sleep late.
—Bajan proverb

We all deserve some "comfort" in our lives, but sometimes we allow it to keep us from working toward our goals. Even though we desire more, we don't "hurt" enough to get up and change things. We lose our motivation, having become lulled by familiarity with our current situation.

Let's ask: Have we persuaded ourselves into accepting things as they are, when in fact we feel dissatisfied or unfulfilled? We'll have to throw off the blanket if we're going to get to work!

On this day, I will take five minutes to talk to my child about complacency: If there is anything he feels complacent about, we will discuss how he feels about that complacency and, if it should be blasted away, how that should be done.

COMMUNICATION

How come people that love you can't read your mind?
—*Pearl Cleage, from her play* Hospice

Our loved ones may come to "read" us rather well, actually—understanding what a certain vocal inflection portends or learning to back off when we put on Billie Holiday. But no one should be expected to guess our every desire, anticipate our mood, or tell us what we need to hear *when* we need to hear it. Our children, in particular, should not have to tiptoe around us or live in dread of our outbursts of sarcasm.

We can avoid wounding or alienating everyone in the house by communicating our needs before things approach the boiling point. "I need some quiet time alone" or telling our mate, "I need a hug/laugh/break/career change/back rub" can keep us from stewing in our juices, feeling alone and misunderstood.

On this day, I will take five minutes and visualize that I have anticipated my needs and articulated those needs to my family.

EVALUATING

Get used to evaluating people; that's how decisions are made.
—Eric V. Copage

Our children will learn later in life that they will be evaluated over and over again. Can they do the job? What are their strengths/weaknesses? Will they buckle under pressure? Do they have anything unique to contribute? And they, too, must learn to evaluate others—both on the job and in their personal lives.

It can only help to develop those powers of analysis early on, which might save them from unsavory influences and unproductive relationships. Evaluating others can also help them remain true to themselves, to their own goals and values, and simultaneously, help them to be compassionate and wise.

On this day, I will take five minutes to ask my child to evaluate one of his acquaintances—what are his interests, what is he good/bad at? Would you want him on your baseball team? Would you want to work with him on a classroom project? Why or why not?

SECURITY

*Security is not an address. It's something you carry
with you wherever you go.*
—Roz Ryan

Who among us *doesn't* feel insecure once in a while?
Our child's developing sense of security can be on especially shaky ground during these turbulent years of
childhood and adolescence. It can be frustrating to a
parent whose reassurance and attempts at ego boosting
seem to mean less than peer acceptance and party invi-
tations. But, as a parent, it is our responsibility to try to
guide our child and show him ways to change and re-
learn the way he thinks of himself.

*On this day, I will try to keep the focus on the positive
aspects as much as possible, and try to engage my child in
activities that provide a newfound sense of competence or
enrichment.*

FAMILY CONFERENCES

*If some important decision had to be made about
school or the house or money, Ma would call a
family conference and the three of us would sit on
the couch and we'd talk. She wanted our opinions,
she told us. I feel it was valuable that she thought to
consult us, to make us feel that we had some say in
our lives.*
—Dave Winfield

Of course, the kids aren't going to make major decisions on their own, but the family conference is a great
way for children to learn about responsible decision
making. They learn how important it is to articulate
their feelings clearly, to reason coherently, and to ne-
gotiate and compromise. Siblings at war with each other
can grow to understand each other's viewpoint. Without
a voice in their own home, children can resort to less de-
sirable, less productive ways to register their presence.

*On this day, I will take time to find some household decision,
no matter how minor, my children
can help make.*

FORGIVENESS

*I'm not proud of a lot of stuff that I have done, but
I'm a really good person.*
—Elaine Brown

We all have things in our lives of which we are not
proud. We are emotional beings, and we sometimes say
and do things out of our own pain or fear or immaturity
that we later regret.

It's vital that we forgive ourselves our misdeeds
and recognize that they do not speak for our entire beings.

By the same token, let's keep in mind that our
children, too, have vulnerabilities and are bound to
make mistakes. It's unfair to brand them with negative
labels. They need and deserve to feel good about themselves; we can show them the way.

*On this day, I will take five minutes to forgive my children
any aggravation they may have caused me, and to forgive
myself for any momentary lapses I might have had toward
them.*

DAUGHTERS

*When in this world a man comes forward with a
thought, a deed, a vision, we ask not how does he
look, but what is his message? The world still wants
to ask that a woman primarily be pretty.*
—W.E.B. DuBois

How do we talk to our daughters? Do we find that our
compliments have more to do with their appearance,
while, with our sons, we more often commend their performance? When the only positive things we say are in
the order of, "Don't you look pretty in that new dress,"
values can get misplaced. Perhaps we need to make
more of an effort to praise our daughter's hard work, her
initiative, her tenacity, her mastery of a skill or a class at
school. Let's make sure she knows that *her* thoughts and
dreams are as valuable as her brothers'!

*On this day, I will make a special effort to praise my
daughter for her thoughts and actions. And if I have no
daughter, I will make a point of complimenting a black female
on something of substance she has done.*

May 9

SELF-CONFIDENCE

What people think of me isn't any of my business.
—Oprah Winfrey

Our decisions and goals as parents are as open to criticism as any other choices we make in life. Friends and family members may carp at our parenting style, proclaiming their own methods and viewpoints to be the wiser way, but are we going to let them determine, say, whether our child is really up to that advanced class? Not to say we should totally stop up our ears to other opinions, but assuming we are attuned to our child's needs and abilities, we need to have faith in our judgment.

On this day, I will take five minutes to affirm my trust in my ability to sort through my options as a parent and arrive at the decisions that are appropriate for me and my child.

NUTRITION

If a child comes to school hungry, the best school in the world won't help.
                                        —Arthur Ashe

Years ago, on a block in New York City where I then lived, I saw a child come out of a store one morning before school with a bag of potato chips and a bottle of fluorescently colored drink. No doubt in my mind—this was breakfast. How frustrating, when you consider that the same dollar or so that bought this nutritionally bankrupt "meal" could have gone for a bowl of oatmeal, orange juice, and a slice of toast at home.

Part of our job description as parents entails nutritional expertise. It's not enough to stuff our child's stomach; those calories have to count for something.

On this day, I will take time to assess my child's diet and make changes that will make it a more healthful diet.

DISCUSSION

I believe in talking with children, taking time with them, taking them to places of interest, doing things together.

—*Maggie Comer*

There are lots of opportunities to stimulate our children's minds. Maggie Comer stresses the importance of simply "making them think about things."

Let's not overlook this significant way to make a positive impact on our children. Let's always be ready to answer questions, ask questions, discuss, and debate. Our children will gain confidence in their ability to process information, to think critically and creatively, and to express themselves—big dividends for a little investment of our time and attention.

On this day, I will take five minutes to talk with my child about something of her choosing, and I will be sure to answer all of her questions thoughtfully.

OPPORTUNITY

*We have to begin telling children the truth, which is
that dignity and survival have been possible for
blacks in the worst of times, which they are not
today unless you let them be.*
—Anthony Walton

As our children learn more of the history of our people
in this country, they should begin to develop some perspective. As discouraged as we might get about condi-
tions in America today, it is undeniable that we have a
far greater range of choices available to us. We do have
a say over our own bodies, and, as was not the case with
our ancestors, we can be educated.

Out of respect for those who came before and out
of respect for *ourselves,* we must commit to realizing our
individual potential and making our contribution to the
legacy of hope.

*On this day, I will take five minutes to talk to my child about
the opportunities he can create for himself in today's
America, and the importance of realizing
his full potential.*

INDEPENDENCE

Thirst cannot be quenched by proxy.
—Zairian proverb

Just as we cannot expect others to do our work for us, we cannot do everything for our children. Some may think that being a good parent means simply that they are on hand all the time to handle their child's difficulties and problems, to figure out solutions and free the child of all responsibilities and unpleasant chores. What results is that the parent deprives the child of the opportunity to employ his own energy, imagination, and resourcefulness. The child gets in the habit of expecting others to do his thinking and his work. Instead of being "freed," he actually becomes dependent, inexperienced as he is in fending for himself.

It's fine to want to make life pleasant for our children, but let's make sure we allow them to grow up with a sense of competence and responsibility.

On this day, I will take five minutes to visualize a situation in which I am watching my child work out a solution to a problem. I will imagine not giving my child an answer, but rather helping her find the answer for herself.

PROMISE

*My parents knew how much it hurt me to be the
worst in the family, knew how much I wanted to
succeed, and they spotted some talent in me before
anyone else did, myself included.*
                                                    —Carl Lewis

At first, Carl Lewis resented the way his parents pushed
him. For a time, he had considered himself the untal-
ented child in his family. Fortunately, his parents saw
promise in their son and worked him harder with extra
drills.

Our own children may at times feel down about
themselves. That's where we come in. More than words
are necessary; we'll have to devote some time and energy. We can help them identify the habits that are sabotaging them and set small goals for improvement.

*On this day, I will take time to list three special talents my
child has, and pledge to help him spot them, express them,
and build upon them.*

DISAPPOINTMENT

I don't mean to be one of these people who says everything happens for the best, because when you hear someone say that you are listening to a defeated person.
—Jamaica Kincaid

"Everything happens for the best." We may have shrugged our shoulders once or twice ourselves and uttered those words. Good thing our enslaved and persecuted ancestors did not take them as their motto. Are these words that could have inspired the Civil Rights Movement?

Let's not string these words together and teach them to our children. They are words that bind motivation, that hog-tie the will to succeed.

On this day, I will take five minutes to talk to my child about how to take a situation that didn't work out and use it as motivation for her next task.

TELEVISION

Television cannot be held responsible for our children. Parents can. Parents must.
—*Clarence Page*

Some of us point our fingers accusingly at television and complain that it's giving our children the wrong values. Let's turn off the TV. What sense does it make to expect television to inspire our children into action or to supply them with positive role models? *We* must be their positive role models. *We* must inspire our children into action. But that can't happen when we ourselves are staring at the tube.

On this day, I will not turn on the TV or the radio. I will chat with, play a game with, play catch with, bake with, or participate in something with my child that requires interaction.

ADAPTING

Adapting doesn't mean that you're denying yourself. It's like going undercover, to protect a little flame.
                                        —Neneh Cherry

It's natural to want to feel comfortable in our jobs and our relationships. We may see that a certain decorum is called for in the office; we need not worry that we are untrue to ourselves or our culture when we act accordingly.

On this day, I will take five minutes to discuss with my child an item relating to black pride—kente cloth, for instance, or a family photograph—and suggest that she let that object inspire her to excellence throughout the day.

May 18

DREAMS

*We have to give our children, especially black boys,
something to lose. Children make foolish choices
when they have nothing to lose.*
                    —Jawanza Kunjufu

When we encourage our children to dream, we give
them an investment in the future. And if they have an
investment in the future, they have something to lose,
because they have a stake in the world. Let us allow
them free reign to imagine the possibilities: a neuro-
surgeon, a business tycoon—of course! But also we
must equip them with the tools they will need to feel
that their dreams are possible. When they realize they
have something special going for them, the choices they
make are likely to reflect their sense of ownership in this
world.

*On this day, I will see if there are organizations in my
community that can assist in providing a positive
atmosphere for my child. If not, I pledge to start a small
study group after school or an informal arrangement with
another committed parent or two to take the children to
museums or library programs.*

COLLECTIVE WORK AND
RESPONSIBILITY

*As I move on, I just try to do a little better so I can
help more people. If I can't do that on the job, I do it
as volunteer work.*
— Sharon McPhail

Sometimes it's all we can manage just to keep our lives
running smoothly. How can we give back to our people
without shortchanging ourselves and our families?

We may just need to take stock of what we have to
offer. Money? Time? Professional expertise? Maybe we
can donate old clothes or a used typewriter to the needy
or a plate of brownies to the church bake sale or gather
resources for an after-school program for children.

Promoting the progress of African Americans is
one of our great traditions, and one that we pass on to
our children by showing them the way.

*On this day, I will discuss with my children some way we
can contribute to the community, whether it be
the black community, school community,
or the global community.*

MONEY

*A parent quickly learns that no matter how much
money you have, you will never be able to buy your
kids everything they want.*
— *Bill Cosby*

We cannot feel guilty about this; we can only be resourceful and determined and provide for our children as best we can.

Let's keep in mind: Fancy toys don't ensure success or emotional well-being. It is the parent-child interaction that is key.

*On this day, I pledge to be there for my child, and remember
that my deposits of love and encouragement will pay the
greatest dividends of all.*

DISCUSSION

*The best doctor, best medicine, best antidote for
what ails us is the mirror reflection of ourselves: our
friendships, our bonds, the comfort we seek and the
support we receive from each other.*
—Opal Palmer Adisa

Raising children is a tough business. There are times we
just need to talk, let off steam. Our true friends will understand, so let's be sure to reach out. We may learn
about a compassionate tutor, a fun class at the Y, a ded-
icated teacher at school. We can pick up tips for dealing
with our child through their many, sometimes bewilder-
ing stages. And when we hear *our friends'* problems, we
may not feel so distraught anymore.

*On this day, I will take five minutes to talk to a friend about
parenting. If I do not have such a friend,
I will set about cultivating one.*

TIME

*I like to spend time alone with my children, whether
it's all three of them together or one at a time. When
I team up with one child, I come to understand his
or her individual personality and what that child is
about inside.*

—Bo Jackson

Children need to have us to themselves on a regular basis, so if there's more than one child in our family, we're going to have to become experts at apportioning our time.

Alone with us, our child can express her feelings and talk about her interests without worrying about big brother putting in his two cents. In those precious minutes, there's no competitiveness, no posturing, no bickering. Our child must have our complete attention, however; an hour spent in front of the TV doesn't count. At the same time, there doesn't need to be an "agenda" to our time together.

*On this day, I pledge to find time to focus on each of my
children separately.*

POWER

Sharp ax better than big muscle.
—*African-American proverb*

There has always been much talk among African Americans about power—our lack of it and how to get it. Paradoxically, much has been made about us being a "minority" within the majority, but also the largest "minority" among minorities. The fact is power has nothing to do with the size of a group. In fact, the majority *never* rules. Power has to do with the discipline with which a given minority manipulates key resources—mental resources (education, technology, religion, for instance) and physical resources (financial, natural resources, for instance). The British knew that and ruled the world for a time. We as a group can grow more powerful by using the resources that can never be wrested from us—emphasis on education, intelligent spending, a sense of our destiny—to reach those important resources that are up for grabs.

On this day, I will take five minutes to emphasize to my child that discipline applied to education, finances, and work will ultimately yield power.

CYCLES

*When I'm not hittin', I don't hit nobody. But when
I'm hittin', I hit anybody!*
                                    —*Willie Mays*

Our children will find out what *we* already know—there
are just some days we can't win for losing. Bad luck
seems to follow us everywhere. We shake our heads in
exasperation and check the clock—bedtime yet?

On days like these it's nice for our child to have a
parent who understands. What can we do? A love note
on the pillow, a few bright flowers at bedside, a favorite
dessert or dinner—whatever might bring a smile. Small
gestures can add a sweet note to an otherwise sour day
and reassure our child that she is loved by us and that
tomorrow will be better.

*On this day, I pledge that when my child
is frustrated or on a losing streak, I will do
something to cheer her up.*

FIGHTING

*It takes steady nerves and being a fighter to stay
out there.*
—*Wilma Rudolph*

It's true that we must be fighters, but it is also true that
we must be smart fighters. There are some confrontations that only lull us into thinking we have done something for ourselves or our people. These fights can
deplete us of energy that can be more productively chan-
neled into securing the gains we ultimately seek to
make.

*On this day, I will discuss with my child the idea of
confrontations, and the idea that steady nerves and alertness
and focus will help us to sort out the meaningless scuffles
from fights truly worth taking up.*

LABELING

*Mom's favorite question was, "Boy, why you so
bad?" I tried many times to explain to Mama that I
wasn't "so bad."*
                                            —Claude Brown

Our children's behavior can be baffling. We can yell until we're hoarse, but to no effect. Have we tried to explain our anger and disappointment calmly, holding
back on the accusations and put-downs? Have we allowed them the chance to tell us what's really going on
inside them? Our child may not be able to pinpoint or
articulate the reasons for his actions, but it's possible, if
we're attentive and alert to patterns and developmental
phases, for us to pull them out of the silences.

*On this day, I will pledge not to be critical of my child, but,
when the situation warrants, to be critical of his behavior
only. I also pledge to give him encouragement any way I can
at every opportunity.*

                                                    May 27

SEXUAL ABUSE

*We need men to stop giving consent, by their
silence, to rape, to sexual abuse, to violence. You
need to talk to your boyfriends, your husbands, your
sons, whatever males you have around you—talk to
them about talking to other men. When they are
sitting around talking bad about women, make sure
you have somebody stand up and be your ally and
help stop this.*
—Byllye Y. Avery

And why shouldn't men and women be allies in this?
That means addressing the little sexist comments that
slip out that our boys might be picking up in the playground or on TV. That also means fostering a sense of
self-esteem in both our boys and our girls so that they
neither resort to nor tolerate abusive behavior.

*On this day, if I have a son, I will make sure to tell him that
he should have a healthy respect for members of the opposite
sex. If I have a daughter, I will tell her that she should settle
for nothing less than respect.*

WINNING

You have to know you can win. You have to think
you can win. You have to feel you can win.
                                        —*Sugar Ray Leonard*

A tough sell if our overall attitude is "You just can't
win!" We have to be careful that we're not persuading
ourselves—and those around us—of the futility of our
efforts.

How to kick the negative thinking habit? With
practice! We have to make a concerted effort to see ourselves succeeding at our goals and to replace "I can't"
with "How can I?" Infusing our spirits with positive
thoughts, looking for inspiration and strategy in the
stories of others, and formulating a realistic game plan
can do a lot to keep us moving forward.

On this day, I will take five minutes to instill a winning
attitude in my children by discussing a problem, and trying
to help them find a solution to it.

PARENTHOOD

Momma was home. She was the lighthouse of her community. Within our home, she was an abundance of love, discipline, fun, affection, strength, tenderness, encouragement, understanding, inspiration, and support.
—Leontyne Price

Are these characteristics our children might someday ascribe to *us*? We may not aspire to "lighthouse of our community" status, but we *can* stay tuned in to the ways we interact with our children. If we've been a bit rough lately, we can recognize that and then ease up. We can make a habit of saying "I love you" and "I'm proud of you." If we hear in our voices irritation or impatience, we can take a step back to gather ourselves, or explain our frustration to our children.

On this day, I will take five minutes to evaluate my performance as a parent and pledge to work on any shortcomings.

CHANGE

There will always be men struggling to change and there will always be those who are controlled by the past.

—*Ernest J. Gaines*

Obviously, when we read this quote, we'll want to say we belong to the former group. It only makes sense. Yet it can be a trickier matter putting what *sounds* good into practice. We may not realize we're controlled by the past when we're blaming our childhood woes for our current situation, or when we point to the injustices done to our people as the reason we have stalled in our career.

As Ernest J. Gaines concludes, "Man must keep moving."

On this day, I will take five minutes to examine my attitude towards life and consider whether it is still right for me and whether it has a beneficial or negative effect upon my child.

EDUCATION

I wondered if anyone here had ever expected me to do better than this. Early on they'd told me that I'd do fine. I felt betrayed. High passes were probably what they'd mean by fine—for black scholarship kids.

—Lorene Cary

Author Lorene Cary is talking about her experiences at an elite boarding school. Fortunately, Cary had higher expectations of herself, even while teachers patted her on the back.

This can happen throughout our child's academic career. Standards drop, and a B becomes tantamount to an A when it's on our son or daughter's report card.

Let's make sure to guide our child to set his or her own standards, to pursue excellence in a spirited yet unneurotic way, and to avoid settling for mediocrity.

On this day, I pledge to stay on top of my child's education to make sure she is doing the best that she can.

PRAYER

*Dear God, Thank you for giving my son a strong
mind and a strong healthy body. Thank you for
making him successful in everything he does. Amen.*
                                        —*John E. Copage*

My father composed this prayer and recited it to me and
my brother, Marc, at bedtime when we were children. As
a parent myself, I recite it to my children, ages four and
seven. No matter what has gone on during the day, a
peaceful moment in prayer with our child can end the
day on the right note, reminding us both that we are fortunate and giving us hope for tomorrow. The arguments
and transgressions slip away, and with real warmth and
tenderness, we can kiss "good night" and renew our very
special bond with love and affirmation.

*On this day, I will compose a prayer for my child, or devise
some way that he knows on a daily basis he has my
confidence and is in my dreams,
always, no matter what.*

HOLDING ON

*Most of what I'm saying is you got to hold tight a
place in you where they can't come.*
—*Alice Walker, from her novel* The Third Life of
Grange Copeland

"They" who? They anybody: The bigots, the doubters,
the complainers, the blamers, the permanently angry,
wounded, and reckless. Whomever it might be who
would deplete our spirit and energy.

These are, after all, *our* lives, and we must be prepared to show pride of ownership.

*On this day, I will take five minutes to talk to my child about
the importance of having a spiritual place inside of her that is
sacred and God-given, and tell her no one has a right to move
in that place and befoul it.*

LOVE

*Teaching a child strategies to deal with racism and
the negative feelings about being black that racism
incurs is very helpful. But nothing can substitute for
the love, care, and training that the child needs from
birth onward.*
— *James P. Comer, M.D.*
and Alvin F. Poussaint, M.D.

Given plenty of love and attention, our children will develop a sense of self-esteem that will support them
throughout their lives. It is not necessary, nor is it ad-
visable, say Comer and Poussaint, to bring up race at
every turn. When we compliment a completed homework assignment, or commend the way they help their
younger siblings, we help our children to feel good about
themselves as people. Without the foundation of a
strong, positive identity, an awareness of their strength,
intelligence, and significance—no amount of strategies
will help our children withstand the assaults of racism.

*On this day, I will find something about which I can
compliment my child and tell him how special he is.*

POSSIBILITIES

I am where I am because I believe in all possibilities.
—*Whoopi Goldberg*

Do we see "all possibilities" when we look at our child? If not, then we have willingly shortened our visions, limited our hopes—our child's hopes, too. We've done this all by ourselves—with no white people or school administrators or job interviewer in sight. Unless our child is spectacularly motivated, we may have handicapped her in a big way.

The real issue might be that we've stopped believing in all possibilities for *ourselves*. A shame, but we can work through our negative outlook if we are committed to doing so. Meanwhile, let's be fair with our children and try not to destroy or deny the possibilities that are indeed *theirs*.

On this day, I will take five minutes to talk to my child and encourage her in her dreams, even offering suggestions on how she might make them real.

ADVERSITY

Give advice; if people don't listen, let adversity teach them.
—*Ethiopian proverb*

Of course, we don't want our children actually to harm themselves. And there are some rules that are law, such as no drug or alcohol abuse. It's necessary to be nonnegotiable on issues we deem important.

But our children will also benefit from feeling the consequences of their actions. Being mean to a friend, for instance, can end up with our child feeling hurt and left out—and determined not to be mean in the future.

On this day, I will take five minutes to learn to use some of my child's transgressions as learning experiences and help him to identify smarter behavior choices for the future.

ELOQUENCE

The Jackson kids were taught to be well spoken at all times. We were to be ar-ti-cu-late. I worked hard on my diction so as to impress my dad. He knew it would pay off eventually.
—*Reggie Jackson*

In every meaningful sphere of life one must articulate one's point of view before a person or group of people empowered to make a decision that affects one's life. Our people are masters of The Word, from griots to rappers. Lamentably, too many of our youngsters handicap themselves by rejecting traditional syntax and speech without slang. We must tell them that they will not have the full range of employment and educational opportunities by being articulate only in inner-city speech.

On this day, I will buy recordings or books with writings by one or more of the following people: Malcolm X, Martin Luther King, Jr., Marcus Garvey, or W.E.B. DuBois, to show my child that black people speak in many different ways depending on their purpose and their audience.

ATTITUDE

If you asked me the secret to longevity, I would tell you that you have to work at taking care of your health. But a lot of it's attitude.
—Annie Elizabeth "Bessie" Delany

This thing called attitude can work for us, or against us. It can add to the length, meaning, and quality of our lives, or detract from it. A healthy attitude is worth acquiring, so let's be prepared to do some fine-tuning if ours is lacking and to coax out a positive attitude from our children.

On this day, I will take five minutes to take a look at my own attitudes about things. And I resolve to turn obstacles and setbacks into challenges, and to encourage and help my child to do the same.

CONDESCENSION

I never talk down to my audience.
—Flip Wilson

More often than not our audience is our children, and
when we are busy or tired, perhaps we don't take time to
answer their questions fully. Lord knows they will, according to mood, bombard us with questions and challenge us. But let us try to engage them at their level.
When they ask intelligent questions, let us try to give
them intelligent answers. Our children can greatly develop their conversational style at home, so let's give
them some license to try out their material on us.

*On this day, I pledge to make it known to my children that I
am always open to intelligent conversation and requests for
help.*

AMBITION

My teacher asked me what I wanted to be when I grew up, and I told her a scientist. She said, "Don't you mean a nurse?"
                                        —Mae C. Jemison

We must prepare our children for all the pessimistic, negative, discouraging voices along the way. They will come from people of all races and all ages. Some will "mean well." Some won't. No matter. Our children must listen to the voice *inside* them, which alone speaks to their dreams and desires.

On this day, I will encourage my child to realize one of her dreams.

PHILOSOPHY

*A philosophy of life is something that you work
with. But life is not constant, and so as life changes
one's philosophy should change, too.*
—*Erskine Peters*

The ideas that worked for us ten years ago may no
longer have much relevancy to our life today. As we contemplate change, we can't worry about appearing fickle
or unserious. Nor can we allow others to hold us in place
because *they* are comfortable that way. Our needs
change, our family's needs change, and we have to be
open to the things that will address those needs—
whether we're talking about a new job or career, a new
school for our child, or a move to a different neighborhood.

Let's be sure to stay in touch with ourselves and
make adjustments when necessary so that we are living
intelligently and purposefully.

*On this day, I will take five minutes to examine my
philosophy of life and consider whether it is still right for me
and whether my implementation of it is having a positive
effect on my child.*

IMAGINATION

*Children are imaginative, open, inquisitive and
excited about everything. Isn't it wonderful to have
an audience coming to you with all that open
feeling?*
　　　　　　　　　　　　　　—Faith Ringgold

What we do in response to our child's curiosity and interests can be the difference between an enthusiastic
learner and a bored child. When our child receives our
positive feedback, she will be more motivated to go further. Obviously, the earlier we start the better, but certainly an older child can benefit from our involvement
as well. Perhaps there is a book report or other project
we can discuss with her; perhaps a museum exhibit or
educational television program we can view together. It
can be as simple as sharing a library book of poetry or
planning and sowing a garden together.

*On this day, I will make a list of five ways I can stimulate
my child's intellectual growth, especially in ways that forge a
closer bond between us.*

BLACK PRIDE

*Never let blackness be your problem, but somebody
else's problem.*
　　　　　　　　—Adam Clayton Powell, Jr.

Let's go further. Not only should our blackness not be a
problem for us, it should, in fact, be a blessing, a source
of strength and inspiration. No child should come up
feeling handicapped by race. Yes, there will be ignorance,
insensitivity, and injustice to deal with, but our job is to
fortify our children with a belief in themselves, pride in
their heritage, and the motivation to pursue their goals
regardless of the handicapped minds of others.

*On this day I will take five minutes to discuss with my
child a member of our family or a great man or woman of
African descent.*

COMMUNICATION

*Whenever I try to speak to mama about the things
that weigh deeply on my heart, she changes the
subject. I think it is because she cannot bear to hear
about a pain that she cannot understand, that she
cannot make better.*

—bell hooks

How do we respond when our children try to talk to us
about something meaningful to them? Do we laugh it
off as "kid stuff," belittle their concern? Do we change
the subject, toss off a platitude, or take a superior tone?
Any of the above can close the lines of communication
between us, which can have unfortunate repercussions.
For instance, a daughter who's dealing with new issues
concerning love and sex needs more input than the con-
fused "insights" of her teenage peers. Why miss an opportunity to make a meaningful contribution, to ease
her fears, or provide a sounding board.

Raising our children well means more than dic-
tating; it means learning how to listen.

*On this day, I will take five minutes to consider whether I
am listening carefully enough to my child, and if not, I pledge
to do so.*

GOOD HEALTH

*My mind is like a general, and my body is like an
army. I keep the body in shape and it does what I
tell it to do.*
— *Herschel Walker*

Okay, sometimes our body is disobedient. It foils us despite our best efforts. That shouldn't excuse us for mistreating or ignoring it.

Our children are just starting out in life. It's vital that we teach them healthy habits. After all, would we knowingly offer them a future encumbered by cancer, heart disease, stroke, diabetes, and other ailments? That *could* be in store for them if we get them used to inactivity rather than exercise, and if we encourage a diet of fast food burgers, fries, and sugary sodas.

*On this day, I will take time to assess my child's diet and
make changes that will make it a more healthful diet.*

SACRIFICE

*As a child I noticed the sadness of my mother as
she sat alone in the kitchen at night. Her woman's
work never tickled her to laugh or shout or dance.
But she did raise me to respect her way of offering
love and to believe that hard work is often the
irreducible factor for survival, not something to
avoid. Her woman's work produced a reliable home
base where I could pursue the privileges of books and
music.*

—June Jordan

Perhaps we feel trapped in a certain job or career that is
not bringing us fulfillment. It may lift our spirits to
know that we are making it possible for our children to
learn and stretch themselves to discover their potential.

At the same time we must be careful not to hyp-
notize ourselves into stasis. A closer examination of our
talents and skills, together with a positive attitude, can
point us toward a more rewarding job, career, or endeavor.

*On this day, I will take five minutes to remember that the
sacrifices I have made will result in a stronger black child,
and therefore a stronger black community.*

PACING

Today I try to live a day at a time and do something in that day that's positive.
—Stanley Turrentine

Naturally, we need to make plans for the future, periodically review them, and make necessary adjustments, but we can avoid undue stress by concentrating our efforts on what we can do today. Regarding our children, that "positive thing" might be playing a game, or working on a school project with them. As for our personal goals, that could mean cooking up a healthful dinner, taking thirty minutes to stretch, meditate, or exercise, reading the newspaper, or doing the list making, task setting, or other prep work for a new endeavor that promises financial rewards and/or personal fulfillment.

On this day, I will try to do something positive with my child or in some way inspire her to do something positive on her own.

GUIDANCE

*In life the consequences often come first and the
lessons afterward. In today's era of AIDS and
drugs and violence and too-early and unsafe sex, the
consequences can be deadly or last a lifetime. So
parental communication, guidance and example are
more crucial than ever.*
—Marian Wright Edelman

In making for effective communication with our child,
we must be willing to listen and not just lecture. Also,
let's resist clamming up on our children with tersely
phrased bottom-line rulings and ultimatums. Discussing difficult subjects also gives us the chance to bring
forth factual information our child may not have.

*On this day, I will take five minutes to talk to my child about
AIDS, drugs, violence, too-early and unsafe sex, or another
important topic, and to revisit those topics on an ongoing
basis as needed. In discussing the topic, I will help my child
to frame his questions, to reason well, and guide him toward
sensible conclusions.*

JUNETEENTH

*In the long memory I have cultivated over my
lifetime, the "Juneteenth" of my pre-adolescent years
will always linger. Even in our youth, we were not
only learning our roots, we were also planting seeds:
in our own inherited land, and in our own time.*
—James Thomas Jackson

"Juneteenth" commemorates the day black Texans
learned about the Emancipation Proclamation. For
years it was an official holiday, celebrated with picnics
and gatherings of family and friends. As James Thomas
Jackson testifies, "It meant much more than Negro
Freedom Day, it was Negro *History* Day."

Our special holidays are wonderful opportunities
to celebrate our history. But let's not wait for a specific
date to teach our children about their heritage.

*On this day, I pledge to pick up a book, take in a museum
exhibit, or go through the family photo album. We can create
our own special days to bring family members together and
talk about the family history
that has such relevance for our lives and
the lives of our children.*

CARRIAGE

You carry yourself like a queen and you will draw a king.
—Salt, of Salt-n-Pepa

It all comes down to self-esteem. As adults, we already know that no one can bestow it upon us. At the same time, some of us may see where our self-esteem was whittled down to size through a childhood of indifferent or hurtful treatment. It is ultimately up to us to build it up and guard it from further assaults.

Let's help our children walk tall through life. Let's give them a running start by allowing them to develop a sound and healthy opinion of themselves.

On this day, I will compliment my child on at least one thing he has done.

INDIVIDUALITY

Everybody hears a different drummer.
—Alvin Ailey

These are things our child will not always do: dress as we'd like him to, share our political views, choose the career we had in mind for him, "hang" with the friends *we* would have picked, play the sport we'd hoped he'd play, take up piano instead of drums, be cheerier at breakfast and more organized about schoolwork. We can go on, but space is limited! The point is clear: Our child does not hear *our* drummer nor can we expect him to. But he can dance to his own beat!

On this day, I will list three things that are unique about my child.

PROVINCIALISM

*I will not be satisfied any more with living my life
simply for myself. Other issues are much broader
than my own little world.*
—*Anita Hill*

Any parent reading this book is certainly not living her
life simply for herself. We want the best for our children, so any issue that has an impact on their lives
should be of concern to us—from pollution to politics,
sexual harassment to job discrimination, from the ef-
fectiveness of our schools to drugs, AIDS, and violence
in our community.

Overwhelmed? If each and every one of us did
just a little bit extra, think how far we could go in making this world a better place for our children.

*On this day, I will resist the urge to put on blinders, and
pledge to get more involved with the issues
affecting our world.*

FAULTS

All men have faults. Small men are blind to their
own, and therefore remain small.
                                        —Jean Toomer

As parents, our children look up to us as role models
who will show them the ideal way to live, the intelligent
way to act—in short the way to *be*. It's ironic when you
consider that we ourselves are still growing. We may
have "faults" we're just now coming to terms with, attitudes we'd like to adjust, habits we'd like to shake. We
don't need to be "perfect" people for our children; we
give them a more valuable lesson when we show them
that, as individuals, we have power over ourselves, that
we can change and we can grow.

On this day, I will take five minutes to think of something I
would like to show my children I can
change in myself, then work out a way to follow
through on that.

DISSENSION

Quarrel is not a food which is eaten.
—Ghanaian proverb

Let's take a moment to consider the general climate of our household. Is it marked with constant fighting, arguing, and discord? Neither our children nor we will be able to find much sustenance in such an environment. Not to say there should never be disagreements, which are part and parcel of family life; but our disputes should not dominate the domestic interchange. Healthy debate is one thing; energy-draining home warfare another.

On this day, I will remember to counsel my children and remind myself that there's nothing to be gained in making personal attacks in our family. We should be each other's greatest allies and, as such, search for some resolution or compromise in our dissension.

VALUES

*It's time for strong brothers to stand up and accept
the responsibility of helping our people. Raise your
sons and daughters. Educate them and protect
them. Teach them moral values.*
—*Hammer*

What are the values we teach and how do we teach
them? Our children watch us closely and absorb our
"lessons" without words. We cannot sit on the couch all
day and convince them that hard work counts. When we
are hateful and bitter about life, our children get a dose
of that, too. When we badmouth the opposite sex, we
give our children narrow definitions of people and show
them it is acceptable to trash others on the basis of gender. We have the power to open up their futures by
showing them how to be affirmative, courageous, industrious, and committed individuals.

*On this day, I will take five minutes to think about my
actions and what values those actions are
communicating to my child.*

POLITICAL INVOLVEMENT

*I wish more people would see politicians as public
servants, because that's what they are.*
—Barbara Jordan

Sometimes we lose sight of the fact that it is *we* who put
our mayors, congressmen, councilmen, and governors
in office and *we* whom they serve. Yet our votes alone do
not ensure our representation. We need to make our
voices heard on issues about which we feel strongly, and
we do this by staying informed, by writing letters, making phone calls, attending meetings, circulating peti-
tions, joining committees.

Our children need to see the political process as
an opportunity to effect change. Learning to articulate
and argue their viewpoints will give them confidence in
speaking up for themselves throughout their lives. African Americans have had a strong tradition of activism.
Let's inspire our children to become proud members of
that tradition.

*On this day, I will encourage my children to participate in
civic debate and study issues by bringing up some political
policy or topic at the dinner table.*

EDUCATION

One's work may be finished some day, but one's education never.
—Alexandre Dumas, père

Perhaps we got the idea that "homework" is the penalty for being a child. Did our education end with the last exam we studied for, the last textbook we closed?

There is really no reason to be bored, especially if we are in touch with our changing interests. There may be times where we are naturally eager to know more about nutrition, decorating, or art. Maybe there's a new novel or inspirational biography we've heard about or an author whose earlier books we'd like to check out. Perhaps something our child is studying at school has piqued our curiosity—let's explore things together!

When we stop stretching ourselves, life gets stale and our minds grow dull. Let's give our children the right attitude about learning—it shouldn't stop with the last report card.

On this day, I will talk to my child about at least three new things each of us has encountered today.

SELF-IMAGE

My mother was very big on having a good self-image. I thought of myself as being special and different.

—*Halle Berry*

When was the last time we complimented our child? When did we last solicit her viewpoint or her efforts, or make note of her progress? We are our children's own best pep club when we teach them they are valued and that they have interesting ideas, feelings that count, talents worth developing.

That means taking time to listen to them, to inquire into their days, their schoolwork, and their social scene. It means holding back if we have a tendency to degrade their concerns or criticize. It requires, obviously, more than the occasional pats on the back, but a consistent interest in their development. When we treat our children with respect, we help them to see themselves as worthy, valuable people and to demand respect from the world.

On this day, I will take five minutes to talk to my child about deriving her own satisfaction from her talents and abilities, and doing a good job, always.

OPTIMISM

I look ahead—and I see my race blossoming like the rose. I see schools and churches everywhere. I see love and life everywhere. I see my people everywhere, all over America, all over the world, taking part in the making of a new life. Folks, the sun do move!
—Langston Hughes, from his play
The Sun Do Move

Today, a marvelous quote for the sheer optimism and expansiveness of its vision!

What do *we* see when we look ahead? Does our life, the lives of our loved ones, and the life of our community blossom like the rose? Let's not stunt our growth with pessimism and narrow vision, but make a concerted effort to "see love and life everywhere" when we look to the future.

On this day, I will make a concerted effort to "see love and life everywhere" and to share that vision with my children.

NURTURING

I didn't grow up in one of those families where people sat around and read The Wall Street Journal. *It was quite an awakening when I entered Harvard Business School and found I was competing against people who grew up with that kind of business experience.*
                                        —Marilyn Davis

We needn't be Wall Street tycoons to nurture a child's interest in business, just as we needn't be Toni Morrison to nurture a child's writing talent. If our child shows an aptitude for a subject outside our realm of experience, we can still try to gather as many resources as possible to foster that interest. Teachers may have suggestions; librarians and bookstore owners can suggest age-appropriate books on anything from money to science to art. We can also search out others in the community who might be happy to give advice.

On this day, I will take five minutes to focus on activities or professions that excite my child and resolve to do all that I can so that he might fully realize those interests.

BITTERNESS

You're only bitter if you reach the end of your life
and you're filled with frustration because you feel
that you missed out on something. I know I'm not
going to be a bitter old man.
—Michael Jordan

When we are frustrated, everyone else in our family
bears the brunt of it. If we do not address that frustration in a positive way, then our frustration builds, turning to bitterness. Yes, as parents, we have our
obligations. Sometimes we compromise for the sake of
our children's security, but that should be seen as a positive choice we make.

Let's ask ourselves: How do we want to live our
lives? The images we come up with have to be more than
pipe dreams. Are we working toward these goals? We
may not be exactly where our mental timetable says we
should be, but we cannot permit frustration to make us
lose hope.

*On this day, I will examine my life to see if I am making
time for the goals and dreams that are significant to me. If
not, I pledge to map out
a plan to do so.*

RESPONSIBILITY

*If you have a voice, you must use it for your people
and speak to the world you live in, and if you are
alive you should demonstrate it by using the space
you occupy. You must help shape the world.*
—Bernice Johnson Reagon

Shape the world? Sounds difficult, but we must recognize that our beliefs and actions do have impact. Then we see that we have both choices and personal power.

*On this day, I will take five minutes to talk to my child about
taking responsibility for the literal space she occupies, that is,
her room. I will encourage her to think about how she wants
it decorated and then to take steps toward realizing that
vision and to remind her that she has the power to shape her
world in the larger sense, too.*

SETTING AN EXAMPLE

Children are the clothes of men.
—Yoruba proverb

Just as our clothes can say a great deal about us, so will our children reflect our most closely held ideals, our dreams, and values. If we treasure education, that attitude will be evidenced in our children. If we find meaning and pride in our African-American heritage, that too will be felt in our children's sense of dignity and identity.

If we show—and not just tell—our children how hard work, energy, and perseverance are vital for success, our children are more likely to live by these values.

On this day, I will take five minutes to think about whether I am setting a good example for my child, or if my talk about black pride, black history, and hard work is mere rhetoric.

PATRIOTISM

*This is our home and this is our country. Beneath
its soil lie the bones of our fathers; for it some of
them fought, bled, and died.*
                                        —*Paul Robeson*

As our children learn more about the history of our people in America, they may find patriotism a baffling concept. That's because they focus on what was done to us
instead of what *we* did for this country. We must remind
them that this is as much *our* nation, *our* home, as anyone's, and that our ancestors paid for our stake with
their blood and sweat.

*On this day I will take five minutes to discuss with my child
that African Americans are not visitors here, looking for
hospitality. When we celebrate this day, we do so for the
ancestors who could not, and it is to them as well we pledge
allegiance.*

July 4

VOICES

*Our voices are as much a giveaway as our clothes.
They reveal what we want to be and can't help
being; they show how we earn our keep and save our
pride.*

—Margo Jefferson

Our children hear us, too. How do we sound to them?
Do our voices inspire confidence and warmth? Is our
tone sharp, abrasive, indecisive, flat, and emotionless?
When we address them, is it usually more of a command,
a complaint, or an accusation? Our children realize
when we are derisive of their thoughts and concerns, even
when we don't actually articulate that. Our voices have
power. They can diminish or build, negate or affirm, reveal pride or contempt. They can say, without words,
"You are stupid; I don't respect you; you are a bother to
me—go away." While we may have to take a strong, no-
nonsense tone on occasion, let's, in general, make our
voices speak with love, pride, and respect.

*On this day, I will listen to my voice to see what it is
saying when I am talking to my children, and I will be
ready to make adjustments, if necessary.*

July 5

TOUCH

Not touching someone is a way of rejecting him.
—*James Baldwin*

What do our touches say? Do they grip with anger or caress with love? Are we generous or stingy with our touches and hugs?

Studies have shown that human beings thrive with adequate physical affection. Everyone differs, of course, in the amount they require. Timing is key, too. An eight-year-old boy who breaks out of his mother's arms in front of the school door may have the dearest embrace for her at bedtime.

A touch is so easy. It gets us through the days when we have no time for more involved interaction. It communicates our love and support in the midst of difficult moments.

On this day, I will be sure to give my child a hug.

RELAXATION

*When I got stuck on lyrics, I'd pick up a knife and
start chopping something, just to relax my head.*
                                        —Neneh Cherry

We can get stuck on parenting, too. It can help to tune
out for a while, let the anxieties go, and allow the mind
to roam where it will. Whether we're chopping, scrub-
bing, hammering, or sweeping, we can work off frustration, cool down, and allow for more positive thoughts to
flow.

When we reapproach a difficult situation—perhaps a child who is trying our nerves to the max—we
just might have determined a more creative and constructive way of handling things. It might surprise a
child who was expecting a yell, plus we can get a mean
vegetable soup or stir-fry ready!

*On this day, I will make a list of five ways I can effectively
handle my stress.*

SELF-CONFIDENCE

Not only do I knock 'em out, I pick the round.
—*Muhammad Ali*

Self-confidence. We want our child to have plenty. We worry when he seems to knock himself, to be negative or pessimistic. We are happy to give our praise and affirmation, but we also wish he could find more inside himself.

It may help to think of confidence as a vitamin. In order to have it inside, our child has to be willing to take it in. He gets it from his various accomplishments, skills, and achievements, which help to foster that positive attitude.

On this day, using family, friends, or historical figures as examples, I will take five minutes to talk to my child about understanding that champions win because they actively work at maintaining confidence in themselves, and that all of us have the potential to be champions, too.

FATIGUE

My feet is tired, but my soul is rested.
—Mother Pollard

Scene: Montgomery bus boycott, 1955. Just a quote to keep in mind for those moments we feel physically and emotionally spent. Let us be inspired—like Mother Pollard, whose feet once ached so that things might be better for us—by the good we can accomplish, despite our exhaustion.

On this day, I will take five minutes to discuss with my child black people who came before us—such as Mother Pollard— and encourage my child to draw strength from those people.

July 9

INVOLVEMENT

You can die in the bleachers or you can die on the field. You might as well come out on the field and have a good time.

—Les Brown

True, it may feel safer in the bleachers. We won't get roughed up, won't risk failing and becoming demoralized. But how many of us can honestly say we prefer a lifetime of watching others make their goals while *we* simply warm the bench?

Let's acknowledge we might get knocked down or pushed back on the way to our goals, but if we train right we can be mentally and physically prepared for the assault. Our children will cheer us and benefit by our example. What good is it telling them "Go for it" when we can't inspire them with action?

On this day, I will take five minutes to examine whether I am setting a good example of determination and resilience for my children. If not, I pledge to make adjustments and improve the situation.

ENCOURAGEMENT

My teachers treated me as a diamond in the rough,
someone who needed smoothing.
                                        —Mary Frances Berry

Perhaps we still have not come to appreciate the many
facets of the diamond inside us. Same goes for our children. We can help them with the essentials, nurture in
them a winning attitude toward life, and get them into
habits that will enable them to uncover their own brilliance—but first we have to get them to see the diamond
within. When we treat them as precious, they are more
apt to regard themselves as precious.

On this day, I will find three things my child does well and
tell him about them.

VISION

Just because a man lacks the use of his eyes doesn't mean he lacks vision.
> —Stevie Wonder

Who among us doesn't have some sort of handicap or limitation? Whatever we perceive to be a flaw does not have to hold us back from the vision we have for our lives. It limits us only if we allow it to.

Our children need to understand that limitations do not define them. Other strengths develop regardless, which give their lives beauty and meaning.

On this day, I will take five minutes to talk about true vision.

INDEPENDENCE

Nobody walks with another man's gait.
—Kikuyu proverb

We may want our children to follow in our footsteps, but their feet will take them their own way and at their own pace. Our job is to prepare them, with love, for their journey.

On this day, I will take five minutes to think about
my child—who she is and what she wants to become,
rather than who I want her to be or what
I want her to become.

EXPLORATION

*It is only the narrow people who live for themselves,
who never read good books, who do not travel, who
never open up their souls to permit them to come
into contact with other souls—with the great world
outside.*
—*Booker T. Washington*

Demands on our time, energy, and wallet may cause us
to fall into predictable patterns because it feels too un-
settling or seemingly requires too much energy to
change. But there is a world of riches out there, within
our reach if we aspire to taste them. That good book can
come from the library or the loan of a friend, and we can
start a small book group to have others with whom to
discuss it. We can turn the radio dial to a different station or check out that interesting documentary on public television. We may not be able right now to travel to
the land of our ancestors, but we can prepare a meal of
African foods, put on some African music, and take
turns reading folktales with our children.

*On this day, I will make an effort to broaden my horizons,
enrich my life, and discuss these new pleasures and
possibilities with my children.*

MASKS

*Did Daddies have fear? I never thought so. I
thought fathers were too big and strong to have fear.*
—Diana Ross

Children like to feel secure. They *need* to feel secure, so
that they can be free to play, grow, learn, experiment,
and discover themselves.

Does that mean our children should never spot an
emotion that would render us less than rock steady and
invincible? There may, after all, be plenty of times we do
feel afraid, fatigued, disappointed, uncertain, unhappy,
and frustrated. Some of us may be inclined to try out
our acting skills and smile, smile, smile—but what's
more important is that our children do not see us giving
in to our difficulties, but rather rising up to meet and
challenge them.

*On this day, I will take five minutes to consider whether
I am setting a good example for my children
in my resourcefulness and tenacity when
confronted with a problem.*

IMPROVEMENT

*We ourselves have to lift the level of our community,
the standard of our community to a higher level,
make our own society beautiful so that we will be
satisfied. We've got to change our minds about each
other.*

—Malcolm X

Before we can lift the standard of our African-American community to a higher level, we have to make sure that our own standards are high. That may mean changing our minds about ourselves first. Once we can acknowledge our limitless potential and fully commit ourselves to living the kind of life that has meaning for us, we can touch the lives of those around us.

On this day, I will take five minutes to talk to my child about being open to the beauty of our people. I will also remind my child and myself that by involving ourselves in the betterment of our community, we can stoke our inner fire and confirm our personal power. It's a symbiotic relationship.

July 16

FULFILLMENT

*I've achieved a room of my own—not without
determination. One summer I came up here to this
room and just like a squaw I sat and said I'm not
giving up. I threw out the television, which started
me down the road to victory.*
—*Kristin Hunter*

Writer Kristin Hunter needed a place to work and she
claimed it. Her family cooperated.

We have to be willing to claim the things we need if
we are to be true to ourselves and our dreams. It may be
space we need, or time, or perhaps a small chunk of the
household budget to enroll in a class or start up a business. We might worry about appearing selfish, but sometimes our "worries" are just an excuse to avoid action.

Let's credit our loved ones with some generosity
of spirit and learn to stake whatever it is we need to
pursue our goals. By being fair and flexible, we can
arrive at an acceptable arrangement for everyone.

*On this day, I will take time to evaluate what I need, and
then enlist the patience and cooperation of my family in
attending to those needs.*

DOUTS

*Don't doubt me because that's when I get stronger.
I like to see the smiles on people's faces when I show
them I can do the impossible.*
                              —Marvin Hagler

What happens when *we* hear doubts? Do they reduce us
or make us stronger?

People have all sorts of reasons for saying the
things they do—most of which have nothing to do with
us. Unless we keep constant vigil, we risk becoming
weakened by the doubts of those closest to us.

*On this day, I will take five minutes to talk casually to my
child about strategies—such as visualizing success—for
dealing with naysayers. I will also let him know that he will
always, unconditionally, have my support.*

July 18

CHAMPIONS

*Champs view each challenge not as an
insurmountable hurdle, but as an opportunity for
another victory.*
—Lenda Murray

Are we grooming our child to be a champion? Don't
laugh. Why *not* our child? Champions are not people
who are simply blessed with all the talent. Becoming a
champion usually requires some discomfort—say, getting up two hours earlier to get in the training, the
studying, the writing, whatever one needs to do. Non-
champions roll over and go back to sleep. Three-time
Ms. Olympia Lenda Murray knows—there is no victory without effort and a positive attitude when facing
our challenges.

*On this day I will take time to make a list of five things I
can do to help my child adopt the mind-set that will allow
her to become a champion.*

PURPOSE

*If you jest say, "Lawd have mercy," an don't mean
that, why, ain't nothin gonna hapin. When you
say, "Lawd have mercy," an mean that, you git
credit fur it. It's a bright place in yo livin.*
—Mance Lipscomb

Words are quite meaningless without a sense of purpose
to back them up. We might be true-blue sincere when
we declare: "I'm going to treat my spouse better, listen
to my children more, show more concern toward my
parents, get involved in my child's school, my community, go to church more often, try to live more health-
ily"—but unless we are ready to put some effort toward
our cause, our words are mere babble.

*On this day, I will take five minutes to talk to my child about
the idea of committing to turn words into actions, desires into
results.*

July 20

CORRECTION

An error means a child needs help, not a reprimand
or ridicule for doing something wrong.
—Marva Collins

Errors give us a chance to learn and grow. Our child is no exception. Let's ask, though—is he learning while we are yelling at him? Or is he merely absorbing our anger and threats?

On this day, I will take five minutes to remember that, when correcting my child, my goal is not to diminish him or put him on the defensive. On the contrary, I want to allow him to recognize his misstep and find a better way to make a wiser choice next time.

AIDS

*When the teacher gives a class on AIDS, the
students start laughing and make fun of it.*
—sixteen-year-old New York City student

Schools cannot, and indeed should not, tackle the subject of AIDS alone. Parents *must* join in. This is not to suggest that parents need to endorse pre-marital sex, intravenous drug use, and other behavior that can lead to AIDS. But if we can make our children understand that AIDS must be taken seriously, then it might be easier to encourage them to make disciplined decisions regarding the disease. If we can do that we will have begun to do our job as parents.

*On this day, I will take five minutes to talk with my child
about AIDS, its transmission and prevention, and
encourage an ongoing dialogue.*

EXPERIENCE

Some people might think I've lost a step since I'm getting older, but I've really gotten a little faster. I understand the court now.
—Zina Garrison

With youth comes great exuberance and enthusiasm. Our confidence level is high. As we age, it may feel like we're slowing down. There have probably been some rejections, some disappointments. At the same time, we are better attuned to our temperament, our strengths, our likes and dislikes. We have found ways to adapt to our shortcomings and we've learned how to pace ourselves. We are better able to determine which routes potentially offer fulfillment and which are dead ends. We can channel our energy better. We understand the court now.

On this day, I will take five minutes to reflect on the personal advances I've made. I will put those in my asset column and draw upon them to make meaningful life decisions, and to apply my effort and energy with greater accuracy and assuredness.

PREJUDICE

*When I did encounter prejudice, I could hear
Mother's voice in the back of my head saying things
like, "Some people are ignorant and you have to
educate them."*
—Dr. Benjamin S. Carson

Some African Americans believe it is ignoble to try to
educate bigots. It's not. Of course, there is nothing
wrong with saying you have neither the time nor incli-
nation to educate the ignorant. But unfortunately, they
are sometimes directly between us and the thing to
which we aspire, say a promotion. What *can* we do? We
don't need to bend over backward to show a prejudiced
person we are worthy. At the same time, we need not
waste our energy and mental space on starting a war that
will not ultimately serve our purposes.

*On this day, I will discuss with my child the idea that you
don't have to love or even like everyone
with whom you form an alliance.*

GOOD AND EVIL

God created no man evil.
—Swahili proverb

No evil child, either! This idea is part of our heritage, yet sadly, some of our people seem to forget it. We have heard parents emphatically scold their child, "You're bad!" We have seen parents roughly tug on their child's arm, and worse.

Our verbal and physical abuse in the guise of discipline is wrong and sends our child the message that they are defective, undesirable, a "problem." Can we really afford to brand our child as "evil"? Let's use only positive terms when addressing our children; they will have enough to deal with.

On this day, I will praise my child at least one time.

PREPARATION

My father believed—and it is the validity of these beliefs which has served my life and work—that the most important step in moving toward any goal was to be prepared for opportunity when it presented itself.
—Whitney M. Young, Jr.

Meeting an opportunity unprepared is like finding the right door, but without the key. If, for example, our high-school-age child anticipates a career in television news, he should take classes in journalism and speech, get involved in the school newspaper, look for a college that has a respected communications department, try to get part-time jobs related to his field (at a newspaper or radio station, say), *watch* television news and read up on respected contemporary broadcasters (there are magazine pieces on Bryant Gumbel and Charlayne Hunter-Gault at the library). Our child must know: No one succeeds by vague desire alone.

On this day, I will take five minutes to talk to my child about her ambitions, and try to see if she has a sense of how she might make them a reality.

REFUELING

*Parenting is a lifetime proposition, and sometimes I
get so tired.*
—Miriam Decosta-Willis

Having children seems to entail virtually nonstop demands on our mental, physical, and emotional energy.
Even the most devoted and enthusiastic parent needs
time to stop and refuel. We should not feel guilty. Taking the time and space we need helps us to be better parents, to reenter the fray with greater composure, humor,
and perspective. Our children will appreciate our good
mood—and *we* will appreciate our children!

*On this day, I will make a list of five activities that restore
and replenish my spirit. There might be small daily things I
can do now (luxury baths, yoga stretches, painting), as well
as more time-consuming getaways (museum visits, movies
with friends, or a couple of hours at a favorite café or park
with a good book)
to fit into my schedule later.*

LEGACY/TRADITION

*A child must have a sense of selfhood, a knowledge
that he is not here by sufferance, that his forebears
contributed to the country and to the world.*
                                              —*John Oliver Killens*

No one did us any "favors" by giving us our rights as citizens of this country. Today we seek no "favors" either. Our children cannot grow up feeling that they are seated at the table out of the benevolent behest of others. Their chair, their place at the table, was bought and paid for by their ancestors here. They can sit up straight and, with dignity, demand the respect they are due and contribute in their own way so that future generations have both that sense of selfhood Killens talks about and that sense of *belonging* as well.

*On this day I will take five minutes to talk to my child about
black people who contributed to the building and prosperity of
this country.*

DISCRETION

*Why do black folks habitually begin negative
statements with the following: Black men are . . .
Black people are . . . We are always defining
ourselves. And in front of the kids.*
—Carole Stewart McDonnell

We have to acknowledge this: Some of our worst stereotypes are the ones *we* use to label our people.

No doubt we will go on talking among ourselves
about issues that involve and concern us. But how we
talk with our spouses, lovers, and adult friends is not fit
for children's ears unless we curb our tongue and omit
the negative stereotypes and blistering condemnations.
After all, how should our young son feel when we blast
black men as this or that?

*On this day, I pledge to define our people in positive terms,
and spare my child the unhealthy habit of demeaning our
people with unfair and reckless words.*

July 29

FAITH

My faith in God will keep me strong and I'll always continue to push forward and strive to be the best person I can be. When I fall off course, I'll reach out to God and he'll help me get back on course. God is always there for you.
— *Randall Cunningham*

African Americans have long had a strong spiritual orientation, regardless of our individual beliefs. That intense relationship with God, or a Higher Power, has gotten us through some rough days and has allowed us hope. While we continue to fight and function and strive, our spiritual source can give us the strength to carry on in a positive and wholesome direction.

On this day, I will take five minutes to talk to my child and remind him of the divine within himself and that through him the divine manifests itself.

RISK

*When I was growing up, my mama taught me that
anything worth doing in life should be a little scary.*
                                              —Terry McMillan

It's easy to see why we'd counsel a "safe" career and con-
servative choices. Perhaps that route worked for us. But
what if our child's temperament and ambitions point
her toward a goal that could mean years of struggle and
discomfort? Do we try to discourage her or can we offer
our emotional support? Whether she aspires to be an
Academy Award–winning actress or Supreme Court
justice, do we dampen her enthusiasm by warning her of
the "realities" of life, or by assaulting her self-
confidence with reminders of past defeats and mistakes?
When we consider the alternative—a life defined by limitations on what we can do and be—"scary" gets put
into perspective.

*On this day, I will take five minutes to think about whether I
am projecting my own fears onto my child and making them
part of her legacy. I will meditate upon her talents and desire,
and pledge not to deny her the satisfaction of the struggle
and its rewards.*

July 31

LEADERSHIP

*We must tell our children, "You are the future
leaders of this country."*
—Eric V. Copage

A white acquaintance who had been educated at elite
private schools once told me that students were taught
this message early and reminded of it regularly. It stands
to reason that when you hear repeatedly that you are
part of an elite and destined to be a leader, you start to
scale your dreams and ambitions to match.

There is just no reason on God's earth why *our*
children should not hear this message, too. As the idea
becomes ingrained, it can guide them in the choices
they make and exact a sense of responsibility and the
moral imperative to succeed.

*On this day, I will tell my child that he is the cream, not just
of America's crop, but of the world.*

ACCEPTANCE

*There's no place in the world where you can not be
perfect and still be secure, except with your parents.*
—Anita Baker

Perhaps we can remember what it feels like to bring
home a disappointing grade, to fail to make a wide-open
shot that would have tied the game, or to feel like a social misfit. How our parents responded to us may have
set the pattern, good or bad, for how we react to our own
children's frustrations and shortcomings.

We can learn to give our child space—space to
succeed and space to fail. It is the most valuable gift that
we as parents and caregivers have to give. Some failure
will lead our children on the path to success. Other failures will simply be a run of bad luck. Regardless, letting
them know that they don't have to be perfect will give
them the confidence to seek perfection.

*On this day, I will take five minutes to think about whether I
am giving my child enough space and support to have the
confidence to try her very best.*

CHARM

I never was, nor ever will be, personally popular.
—W.E.B. DuBois

DuBois admitted that, even in childhood, he found it difficult to approach others. Despite this, he came to command a great deal of respect and attention because he developed his inner resources.

Our children don't need to win popularity contests in order to live meaningful and gratifying lives, but they do need strong minds and iron wills. Though taciturn, DuBois was confident of his intellectual abilities and determined that his ideas be articulated.

On this day, I will take five minutes to talk to my child about personal charm and, using family, friends, or historical figures as examples, show that while it can smooth the way, the most important elements to success are hard work and high standards.

CREATIVITY

We are all creative, but by the time we are three or four years old, someone has knocked creativity out of us.

—Maya Angelou

Maya Angelou elaborates: "Some people shut up the kids who start to tell stories. Kids dance in their cribs, but someone will insist they sit still."

We need to give our children as many opportunities as possible to express themselves creatively, and we must reward them with positive feedback. That might translate into allowing that block sculpture to command the living room for a day or two, or stringing up a clothesline "art gallery" for our youngest's finest works. It might mean putting down the dish towel to give our full attention to our older child's poem, rap, or essay for school.

On this day, I will be on the alert for creative expressions in my child, and I will enthusiastically acknowledge them.

KILLING

We lose more lives annually to the crime of blacks killing blacks than the sum total of lynchings in the entire history of this country.
                                                    —Jesse Jackson

Think about it: According to the National Center for Health Statistics, 48 percent of black men between the ages of 15 and 19 who died were shot. (The figure for white men is 18 percent.) What to do? There is no easy solution. In fact, there probably is no *one* solution.

But one thing is for sure: Whatever action or actions taken will require the urgency, intensity, and perseverance that guided us out of slavery and that fueled the Civil Rights struggle. We should not fret, however; the way to return the joy of childhood to black youngsters is well within our reach. As Jesse Jackson has pointed out, "What faces us today is preventable. It is within our power to change our behavior."

On this day, I will take five minutes to talk to my child about nonviolent ways of resolving conflicts.

HOLDING ON

*Who wants to live with one foot in hell just for the
sake of nostalgia? Our time is forever now!*
—Alice Childress

Whatever our personal "hell" might be—an ex-spouse
who was unfaithful, failed career ambitions, or a childhood of abuse—we cannot keep it a part of our life today. Maintaining that pool of misery for the purpose of
dipping into it on a regular basis can only sap our self-
esteem or distract us from more positive pursuits.

Similarly, let's help our children to let go of past
hurts. Being able to recognize and enjoy the positive aspects of life and identify things that give them pleasure
can help our children focus on the present and have
hope for the future.

*On this day, I will list with my child five things that she likes
to do, things that give her pleasure.*

August 6

PARENTHOOD

*Fatherhood is responsibility, it's definitely humility,
a lot of love and the friendship of a parent and child.*
—Denzel Washington

Parenthood requires a delicate balance. We are at once
authority figures and friends. While we are the ones who
set limits and impose order over our domain, we are also
the ones who must foster in our child a strong, independent mind. When we respect their feelings, solicit
their opinions, nurture their talents, and encourage
them to stretch to their potential, we cement a bond of
friendship.

*On this day, I will keep in mind that while discipline is
important, so too is the warmth and generosity of spirit
we share with any loved one.*

POSSIBILITIES

*Failure to recognize possibilities is the most
dangerous and common mistake one can make.*
—Mae C. Jemison

Sometimes we are so mired in our current circumstances that we blind ourselves to the possibilities that are always there. Or, if we do glimpse them, we quickly convince ourselves that it would be far too difficult, if not impossible, to make them work. Let's first determine the dreams we are willing to work for and then figure out how we can make them reality.

*On this day, I will talk to my child about a dream of his.
And we will put that dream and the steps
to attain it on paper.*

FINDING GOOD

Find the good. It's all around you. Find it,
showcase it and you'll start believing in it.
—Jesse Owens

Sometimes children can be just plain contrary. Point out the good and they are quick to indicate the bad. Still, we need to persevere, because negative poses don't have to stick.

It helps if we parents put forth a positive attitude. That can sometimes be tricky, when times are tense or tough for us. A friend in difficult circumstances got a boost out of nightly jotting down five good things that had given her pleasure or gratification that day—anything from reading a story with her child to making a pot full of nourishing soup to cleaning up her desk. Being able to pinpoint the good we do and find in life can work wonders.

On this day, I will ask my child about five good things that happened to her, so that she might get in the habit of looking for good to happen to her.

BLACK PRIDE

One does not become great by claiming greatness.
—Xhosa proverb

Yes, we can point to our heritage and beam with pride, but it does not follow that we can sit back, indulge in self-destructive habits, abuse our spouses, neglect our children, eschew work and discipline and compassion, and still claim greatness. That title has to be earned, by each and every one of us.

Let's make sure, when we talk about "Black Pride," that we exhibit the kinds of qualities of which we can indeed be proud.

On this day, I will take five minutes to discuss with my child an item relating to black pride—kente cloth, for instance, or a family photograph—and suggest that he let that object inspire him to excellence throughout the day.

KINDNESS

*My dad could be tough; Lord, he was tough when he
had to be. But he could always smile, no matter how
hard the times were.*
—*Reggie Jackson*

Being tough, being warm. It's the warm part that makes
the tough part work. If, after all, we show our children
nothing but sternness—enforcing rules, exacting order
and discipline—then they are apt to resent it and, in
time, challenge us.

*On this day, I will take five minutes to remember that every
child needs lots of smiles. It is the smile that makes the child
feel good, loved, warm, secure, and, ultimately, interested in
doing right. I pledge to bestow smiles upon my child
generously.*

SELF-RESPECT

*My mother was a great woman. She went through a
lot of suffering to bring the twenty of us up, but still
she taught us to be decent and to respect ourselves,
and that is one of the things that has kept me going.*
—Fannie Lou Hamer

It's difficult teaching manners to an adult if he's never
had to say please or thank you as a child. Same with
self-respect—it's wise to start young. Mere commands
to "respect yourself" don't carry much weight. We have
to be willing to consider our child's feelings, honor his
need for privacy, encourage his ideas and interests. A
good foundation built at home will carry our child out
into the world and "keep him going" through his tough-
est times.

*On this day, I will make a list of five ways I might give my
child a more secure emotional foundation.*

August 12

FREEDOM

Freedom without equality is not enough. . . . In freedom, you simply have the option to push from out to in and from in to out. But with equality, it's about moving up. It's about equity and parity, as opposed to welfare and charity.
                                                    —Jesse Jackson

We are "free" now and look at the problems within our community: violence, crime, uncared-for children, drugs. Equality can indeed be achieved, *if* we are willing to seize it, fight for it, make it work for us and others. It means individual and collective effort toward accomplishing our goals. As we acquire power and create opportunities, we give incentive to others in our community and hope to those children who need it most.

On this day, I will take five minutes to talk to my child about what she is doing to insure our equal place in the world. Being diligent is a good first step.

BEARING

I carry myself the way I do because I am royalty within myself.

—Iman

It can seem trivial when there are so many serious concerns in our community, but how we carry ourselves affects both how others see us and how we see ourselves. Many of our ancestors knew the significance of carrying themselves with dignity in the face of great oppression. Today, too many of our children show, not dignity, but a glaring, scowling face to a world that has far more opportunities than the one our forebears faced.

We need to work with our children at an early age and to help them see that their bearing affects not only how others perceive them, but, most of all, how they see themselves.

On this day, I will tell my child that if he stands tall, it can help to reinforce good feelings about himself.

GIFTS

We start with gifts. Merit comes from what we make of them.

—Jean Toomer

In reading through many of the quotes in this book, it becomes quite clear that successful people credit their accomplishments to dedication and hard work. From athletes to artists to businessmen, those who have achieved have done so not simply because of some spectacular talent, but because they were driven to develop and hone their gifts, to weather failure, and to be tenacious in their pursuits.

Our children cannot be duped into thinking they have no chance if they are not the best player on the team or the smartest kid in class. They must know that Michael Jordan did not, at first, make his high school team, that Dave Winfield wasn't the best player in his youth, nor was Carl Lewis the fastest runner.

On this day, I will take five minutes to talk to my child about her gifts, and remind her that it's up to her to make the best of them.

August 15

RELAXATION

*Go within every day and find the inner strength so
that the world will not blow your candle out.*
—*Katherine Dunham*

In the hectic pace of our lives, taking time to "go
within" can be the first thing to go, squeezed out by
laundry, lunch making, or any of our myriad daily tasks.
When we habitually resist allotting some private time to
assess our current situation, to review our goals, and to
take a reading of our fulfillment quotient, we can begin
to lose track of things. Our dreams can seem to slip
away; our vision for our lives gets clouded. We need to
keep in touch with ourselves, to renew our inner resources of faith and optimism, and to dip into these re-
serves as often as we need to.

*On this day, no matter how full this day is, I will take five
minutes to be alone, take a deep breath, and relax.*

August 16

PACING

*It's one big race that you have to run. It doesn't do
any good to show early speed; it doesn't do any good
to coast in the beginning and save for a kick.*
                                    —Bryant Gumbel

If we coast too long, at *any* point, we can lose momentum and the psychological edge it takes to win. No question, pacing ourselves can be tricky. There may be times we'd like to pull ahead, but other people or obstacles get in our way.

It helps to assess ourselves on a regular basis, to make sure we're not lagging so much that we're going to defeat ourselves. The same thing can be applied to our children; we need to get them off to a good start in their education so they gain the kind of confidence and competence it takes to hang in there down the stretch when the competition is fiercest.

*On this day, I will take five minutes to consider whether I
am pushing my child too hard or not hard enough in his
school or other areas.*

SHARING

When I used to take the children to my readings,
they never cried. At a very early age they had a
sense of what it was I was doing.
—Sonia Sanchez

Sonia Sanchez found a way to bring her children into
her writer's life, and it's unlikely that they will forget the
early experience of hearing their mother's work read to
them and others.

There are numerous ways we can relate to our
children. There will be times to get down on the floor
and do jigsaw puzzles, and times we bake a pie together.
But we can also try to share the work we do or the hob-
bies *we* enjoy. Our children will appreciate the effort we
make.

On this day, whether it's a short visit to the office or the
vegetable garden, I will not overlook all the ways I have to
share my life and strengthen the bonds
I have with my child.

August 18

RECOGNITION

One of the simple things that kept me going was getting my picture in the paper. Maybe my peers weren't playing tennis, but they weren't getting in the newspaper, either.
—Mali Vai Washington

Rising tennis pro Mali Vai Washington can attest to the importance of recognition. While parents and child psychologists alike debate the merits of rewarding children with money or "treats" for good grades and achievement, a simple theory reigns in *our* household— that, in life, rewards are possible through hard work. That might mean a soccer trophy, taking an onstage bow at a musical recital, election to an honors class, or a picture in the newspaper recognizing an exceptional performance in a sport or academic program. These rewards boost confidence, which can then spill over into other areas of a child's life.

On this day, I will compliment my child on something she has done well.

PRIORITIES

*If black America were as interested in power as we
are in basketball, we would dominate.*
—*Nikki Giovanni*

Ouch! But Giovanni goes on to describe us as "potentially the tone-setters of the world. . . .We can do anything we want to do," she asserts. So, it seems to come down to priorities.

As parents, providing for the optimal mental, emotional, and physical growth of our children is at the top of the list. Our children, however, may need some help understanding the concept. Developing to their full potential will not see them in the playground or in front of the television every spare minute of the day.

If African Americans are to accumulate power, we individually have to commit to acquiring it.

*On this day, using examples from our family, history, or
contemporary life, I will take five minutes to talk to my child
about summoning the discipline to stay en route to goals,
and how one forges alliances with those who can help
move us closer to our goals.*

FRIENDS

Let us gather around our children and give the security that can only come from association with adults who mean what they say and share in deeds which are broadcast in words.
—Howard Thurman

We are often more concerned about the company our children keep than that which *we* keep. It's crucial that the people we let into our lives share similar values and that they do not abuse or drain us. Just as a flower requires a nourishing (not polluted) soil for optimal growth, our children need this healthy foundation from which to grow. The adult community that surrounds them should reinforce the positive nature of friendship, and provide them with the sense that decency, generosity, wholesomeness, and industry are qualities to value and search for throughout life.

On this day, I will take five minutes to think about the people with whom I associate and ask, "How much do I want my children around them?"

PREPARATION

*If you wait for tomorrow, tomorrow comes. If you
don't wait for tomorrow, tomorrow comes.*
—Malinke proverb

Yes, tomorrow will come, whether we are ready for it or
not. Are we on a course that will enable us to greet tomorrow with composure? Will we be able to take our
child on vacation, sign him up for music class or tennis
lessons, handle school and college expenses? Will we be
able to cope with medical emergencies, live comfortably
in our retirement, provide for our families in the event
of death or disability?

*On this day, I will take five minutes to focus on some aspect
of my life and make sure that when tomorrow dawns, I will
be prepared for it.*

UNITY

*When a man lives a decent life, takes care of his
family, and is a contributing member of his
community, that's not news. Such a man doesn't
get into the headlines.*
—Milt Hinton

What we see on the news or in the papers can demoralize
us if we lose sight of the fact that there are millions—
yes, millions—of African Americans who are striving,
working, succeeding.

To counter the dreary messages, we need to celebrate our progress and nurture hope and faith among
ourselves, and we do that in our interaction and get-
togethers with family and friends. Let us draw inspiration from one another, and allow our children to see
that hope and success are all around us in our African-
American family.

*On this day, I pledge to take five minutes to talk to my child
about the heroism that surrounds him in everyday life and to
recognize and celebrate the strengths and accomplishments of
so many of our people from all different walks of life.*

WHITE PEOPLE

*I have spent over half my life teaching love and
brotherhood, and I feel that it is better to continue to
try to teach or live equality and love than it would be
to have hatred and prejudice.*
—Rosa Parks

Perhaps we are unable to disown all feelings of anger or
disdain toward white people. It can seem perfectly sensible, then, for us to counsel our progeny to trust no
white person. Yet, ultimately, this approach does our
children a disservice, for it prevents our children from
forming relationships and alliances that may be useful
to them down the road in their careers, or friendships
that may be a source of pleasure and enrichment.

*On this day, I will discuss with my child the idea that you
don't have to love or even like everyone with whom
you form an alliance.*

ROLE MODELS

*Just because I dunk a basketball doesn't mean I
should raise your kids.*
—Charles Barkley

Where, after all, is Charles Barkley when the report card
comes home?

Our children naturally draw inspiration from
sports figures, movie stars, and other celebrities, but it is
we to whom they look for daily guidance, love, and support. We are their primary role models. Let's make sure
our encouragement is never in short supply, and that
our commitment to their physical and emotional welfare never lags. No NBA star will be our stand-in at that
parent-teacher conference; only *we* can put forth the
values and ideals from which our child can draw
strength and prosper.

*On this day, I will take five minutes to think about what
kind of role model I am for my child, and if it needs
improvement, I pledge to do that.*

CHANGE

*I looked at this nation's capital and saw that it was
not living up to its potential.*
—Patricia Roberts Harris

Former Cabinet secretary (HUD) Patricia Roberts
Harris was commenting here on her motivation for running for mayor of Washington, D.C. Though she lost to
incumbent Marion Barry, she should be remembered
(she died of cancer in 1985) for her desire to serve and
make a difference.

There will no doubt be numerous areas where we
can make a difference—within ourselves, our families,
our community, our profession. It takes no effort to
complain about what's wrong; it takes dedication and
tenacity to get in there and change things.

*On this day, I will take five minutes to remind myself and
my child that we are as strong as we allow ourselves to be.
We have as much influence as we permit ourselves. Whether
we act on our own or need to gather forces in order to shake
things up, the power rests with us.*

August 26

RESILIENCE

My job is to be resilient. That's why I call life a dance.

— Bill T. Jones

Life offers us all—young and old—sprinklings of adversity and unexpected challenges. Some of us have an easier time than others adapting, but we can all build up the inner resources that make us resilient.

It helps always to be on the lookout for inspiration, whether through learning about our history and the ancestors who showed enormous strength and courage, or through reading about contemporary success stories. Perhaps we only have to look as far as a parent, or a dear friend, who had to contend with misfortune and came through it in one piece.

On this day, I will take five minutes to nurture resiliency in my child, so that she can cope with challenges, and be better able to persevere with her dreams.

COURAGE

*I was brought up knowing that you don't let
anybody get you down and you don't let anybody
get the best of you.*
— *Charlayne Hunter-Gault*

Our children can be particularly sensitive to the opinions of their peers. We must show them the way to look within and to locate and celebrate their many strengths, their talents, and their innate goodness. As parents, we have a special duty to try to build up and reinforce our child's confidence. That means resisting such comments as: "What's wrong with you?" If we encounter behavior problems, let's address the behavior and not take it as the sum total of our own child.

*On this day, I will find something on which I can
compliment my child.*

GROWTH

I think the artist has to be something like a whale swimming with his mouth wide open, absorbing everything until he has what he really needs.
—Romare Bearden

Not just the artist—all of us, and especially our children, need to be "something like a whale." If we do not know all that the world has to offer, we are unable to make truly informed decisions. We may never discover a career path that would excite us or a hobby that would bring us pleasure or an art form that would provide us with an outlet for our creativity.

Let's open ourselves up to all that we need to insure our optimal personal growth.

On this day, I will talk to my child about at least three new things each of us has encountered today.

August 29

BLACK POWER

*It was thrilling to be able to challenge the
circumstances in which black people were confined;
to mobilize and raise consciousness, to change the
way people saw themselves, blacks could express
themselves. It gives you an unshakable confidence in
your ability to make a positive difference.*
—*Kathleen Cleaver*

Our Black Power movement happens daily throughout
our lives. It starts with ourselves, it goes to our children.
We can all learn to feel our power. It may take a conscious and determined effort; we cannot devalue or
overlook the significance of positive action on a small
scale—the one-to-one influence we have on the people
who surround us. When our children feel that their contributions have value, that their perspective and feelings
merit respect and consideration and that their futures
are promising, they do not need to grasp at desperate or
dangerous means to register their personal power.

*On this day, using examples from our family, history, or
contemporary life, I will talk to my child about how
incremental change can be powerful and long-lasting.*

OVERSPECIALIZATION

*Sports can give children a sense of team spirit,
flexibility, individual role playing, and acceptance.
But sports can also create a certain false sense of
accomplishment and a narrow focus on life's
opportunities.*

—*Bo Jackson*

Okay, somewhere out there is the next Bo Jackson. Yes, it could be your child. Does that mean his intellectual and social development should be sacrificed in the name of his athletic abilities? Bo Jackson's mother knew better; she pushed education as a means to success. Her son's future was too important to gamble on sports; the man would have been a success at any profession.

*On this day, I will take five minutes to think about the
direction my child is going in. Is he putting too much
emphasis in one area? Am I pushing him in one direction to
the exclusion of any others?*

August 31

HERITAGE

I am not tragically colored. There is no great sorrow
dammed up in my soul, nor lurking behind my eyes.
I do not weep at the world—I am too busy
sharpening my oyster knife.
—Zora Neale Hurston

Probably the first thing our children learn at school regarding their heritage comes near Dr. Martin Luther King Day. In essence, it's about how our people were denied basic rights as citizens and how the Civil Rights Movement helped to change this. Right away, then, they get a sense of sorrow in being African-American, and this is built upon as they learn more about our history here. But there is joy and genius and strength in being black, and we have to make it our business to celebrate those aspects with our children.

On this day, I will take five minutes to help my child focus on the joy and blessings of being of African heritage. I might share with him the rich designs of kente cloth and discuss their meanings, or just take a short walk with him, look at the clouds and flowers and let him know there is a special joy in being alive.

PATIENCE

Patience has its limits. Take it too far and it's cowardice.
    —George Jackson

Seems like people are always telling us to be patient. Sometimes we've just got to tune them out and make things happen. That might mean making a dozen phone calls to see to it that our child is placed into a more appropriate class or gets whatever testing or support would benefit him.

We cannot afford to be too patient when it comes to our children. Their years build upon each other, and we must see to it that none are thrown away in our desire to be "patient" so that others do not have to pay attention or expend some energy.

On this day, I will list three things I can do today to help my child on the road of life.

RESOURCEFULNESS

*I borrowed a typewriter from my next door neighbor
and changed my life.*
—Vertamae Smart Grosvenor

Vertamae Smart Grosvenor was looking for something creative to do. It couldn't cost anything, and she had to be able to do it at home. The result of her yearning for creative expression was a cookbook that yielded opportunities she had never dreamed of.

What did it take? Resourcefulness, certainly. Determination, too, since once she borrowed that typewriter she did not let it collect any dust.

This is a lesson for our children and ourselves. There may be times we'll feel stuck in a rut, with no alternatives. By exploring our needs and desires and refusing to be deterred, we can find solutions. The results may not bring immediate or monumental change, but are bound to give us new satisfaction and impetus to do more.

*On this day, I will take five minutes to discuss with my child
something he wants to do and ways in which he can go about
getting it done.*

SCHOOL

A school system without parents at its foundation is
just like a bucket with a hole in it.
—Jesse Jackson

When our children get to be school age, we must remain
as active and vigilant in their lives as ever. We must
make certain our child is put into the best, most stim-
ulating classes, that his teachers are being both fair and
encouraging. We must pitch in in the classroom and
show up at the meetings. We must check the homework, call the principal, and, if necessary, take time off
work to sit outside the principal's office until we are seen
and our concern is addressed. We must be willing to
make a commitment of time, resources, or energy when
that is required.

That very first day of school, we are not kissing
our child good-bye and sending him off alone on a journey: We are embarking, hand in hand, in a partnership
that must remain strong if it is to be fruitful.

*On this day, I will take five minutes to evaluate how I might
better support my child at school and be
a more effective advocate for him.*

INTERACTION

De church bells sometimes do better work dan de
sermon.
—*African-American proverb*

Occasionally we lose sight of the fact that positive, pleasant interaction with our children is so much more effective than hours of lecturing, scolding, and preaching. When we praise their curiosity, their performance at school, their interesting thoughts and ideas, our children are encouraged to repeat this positive behavior. But if the only time we acknowledge our children is to chastise them, you can bet they'll see what else they can do to make us pay attention. This automatic "acting out" can brainwash our children into seeing themselves as "bad apples" or persuade them (and us) that they possess some personality defect. When our compliments are voiced with enthusiasm and pride, our children learn how to make their existence felt in productive, pleasurable ways. What child wouldn't prefer a smile to a shout?

On this day, I will take five minutes to take note of all the wonderful things my child says and does, and share praise with her.

PREPARATION

*Your child does not belong to you, and you must
prepare your child to pick up the burden of his life
long before the moment when you must lay your
burden down.*
                                    —James Baldwin

The problem comes if we have not done our job well as
parents and, as the burden shifts to our child, he is unable
to manage it with ease. He may fumble; he may get into
the habit of grumbling about its weight; he may make excuses and cast blame for his inability to carry it well.

One big thing we can do is encourage and nurture academic success; lacking that, our child can be
tremendously frustrated as we push him out of the
nest. Along with opening doors to college and career,
it gives him a sense of accomplishment and the knowledge that he can apply himself and succeed.

*On this day, I pledge to give my child practice in such life
skills as thinking critically, learning the value of money,
and taking responsibility for his actions. These are lessons
that prepare him to make smart decisions later and to
carry himself well out into the world.*

September 6

PERFECTIONISM

*Most people are so hard to please that if they met
God, they'd probably say yes, she's great, but . . .*
—Diana Ross

Some days, there's just no pleasing us. We pick at the way our child eats, dresses, grooms himself, plays, and studies. If we make a regular habit of this, our child soon becomes demoralized.

We need to stop and listen to ourselves. Is there a better, less punitive way of getting their elbows off the table, their sneaker laces tied, their radio turned down?

On this day, if I find myself carping at my child I will count to ten and try to handle the situation firmly, but calmly, with an aim toward helping her make better decisions in the future. And when she does something good, I will be sure to praise her with enthusiasm.

September 7

HEALTH

Whatever genes we inherit does not mean that we cannot improve upon the script that was predestined for us.
—John E. Copage

Our parents and grandparents may have had trouble with heart disease or high blood pressure. That should not imply that we are doomed to suffer the diseases that plagued them, but that we should heed the warning and make appropriate life-style adjustments. That means dietary changes, exercise habits, and necessary medical care (as in mammograms, or blood pressure and cholesterol evaluation).

Let's acknowledge the importance of our family health history when we look at our children, and follow through as we plan our menus, our checkups, and our leisure time.

On this day, I will take time to assess my own and my child's diet and physical activity; I pledge to make changes to include more physical activity or a more healthful diet, if called for.

SELF-IMAGE

I've always felt blessed to look the way I look, to have the bones I have and the richly dark brown skin. Thank God for my mom and dad.
—Judith Jamison

Can *we* look in the mirror and say we feel blessed? Can our children?

Perhaps there are changes we'd like to make—weight loss, a new hairstyle. It helps to be able to separate that which we are willing and able to change, and that which we cannot (our height or bone structure, say).

How unpleasant to go through life feeling dissatisfied. Let's instead tap into that aspect of our heritage that has celebrated individual style—style that emanates from within and is manifested in the way we carry ourselves, the way we laugh, the way we love and live.

On this day, I will find something about which I can compliment my child and tell her how special she is.

September 9

RACE

If I want to say, "I see a bus full of people," I don't have to say, "I am a Negro seeing a bus full of people."

—Amiri Baraka

While we are proud of our culture, we cannot lose sight of the fact that we are part of a larger enterprise: We are human beings. When we go for a hike with our child, we take pleasure in the experience. Let's not imbue every act and discussion with our children with racial significance. Sometimes we've all just got to *be*.

On this day, I will find something of beauty and joy in the world and share it with my child.

September 10

STRESS

Breakfast was about the best part of the day.
Everyone greeted each other in the morning with
gladness and a real sense of gratefulness.
—Edna Lewis

How did we greet the day today? With gladness, or a grumble? Okay, not all of us are morning persons. Still, when we look at the day before us, it helps to assume a positive attitude. We can help the day get off to a smoother start by doing as much advance work as possible the night before—packing lunches, laying out clothes, setting the breakfast table. Our children thrive on a sense of order and regularity, and we've all heard how a balanced breakfast is beneficial to their performance at school.

Why *start* the day with stress? How much more pleasant to have the time to pull ourselves together with ease, enjoy our whole-grain cereal and fresh fruit, plan our day, and kiss our children.

On this day, I will do something to make tomorrow less stressful. For example, I might lay out breakfast dishes or my child's clothes the night before.

STRUGGLE

Any fight and every fight is important.
—Joe Louis

... Just as each test, each homework assignment, each book report, and each school year are important.

A child will have an easier time of it if he or she sustains her momentum through school. Letting down in one subject or for one semester or school year can have undesirable consequences. Lower grades can be demoralizing and cause a block in our child's mind against that subject or against school in general. She might also get into the unfortunate habit of not trying as hard as she can and adopt the status of "underachiever."

Like a boxer in training, our children must prepare well and live in a healthful manner (proper rest and nutrition) for each and every match.

On this day, I will take five minutes to consider that I am my child's trainer, and as such, play a crucial role in overseeing his progress and telling him when he needs to succeed.

BEAUTY

*My mother adorned with flowers whatever shabby
house we were forced to live in. She planted
ambitious gardens. Before she left home for the
fields, she watered the flowers, chopped up the grass,
and laid new beds. Because of her creativity with
flowers, even my memories of poverty are seen
through a screen of blooms.*
—Alice Walker

No matter what our circumstances, we have the power
to bring beauty into our children's world. It may be our
love of literature, our artistry with flowers or quilt making, our talent at the piano. Our gifts take many forms.
When we tap into the creativity that is in all of us, we
find pleasure and gratification, and teach our children
how they can, too.

*On this day, I will take five minutes to do at least one thing
that makes my child's life more beautiful.*

September 13

READING

*The impulse to dream had been slowly beaten out of
me by experience. Now it surged up again and I
hungered for books, new ways of looking and seeing.*
—Richard Wright

How much do we encourage our children to read? We
may think, sure, we'd love our kids to read more, but it's
possible we're sabotaging their impulses. Does our child
have a comfortable, quiet, well-lit place to read? A selec-
tion of books from which to choose? Do we make regular visits to the library? Do our children see *us* reading
on a regular basis? Are books a popular present for
birthdays and holidays in our home? Do we discuss
books and newspaper stories at the table and encourage
our children to interject their opinions?

Reading does so much for our children; let's
make sure we do all we can to foster a love of books so
that our children's impulse to dream is given full rein.

*On this day, I will take five minutes to discuss with my child
something that either I or he has read.*

WORK

We have been sad long enough to make this earth
either weep or grow fertile.
— Audre Lord

The ancestors have cultivated this earth with their sweat
and blood. We dishonor them not to tend the fertile soil
they left us. It takes hard work, but we must believe that
our toil will bear fruit. We must see to it that the con-
ditions are right for our success. Most important, we
must sow the seed, and weed and water until our efforts
flower.

Our children share in this garden, so it makes
sense that we will want to make them part of our effort.
Let's give them the tools so that they can cultivate a
plentiful harvest in their own lives.

On this day, I will take five minutes talk to my child about
the skills and attitudes it takes to be successful, possibly
using examples from our family, historical figures, or
contemporary celebrities.

September 15

EXCELLENCE

*People will say, "You're a terrific black general." I'm
trying to be the best general I can be.*
—Colin Powell

And people will say to our children, "You're a terrific
black student," as if there is something extraordinary in
an African-American child's high academic achievement.

What others see as being ordinary or extraordinary relates purely to *their* definition of us. Swallowing
their standards can only limit us.

Let's help our children discover their own potential, and not succumb to the criteria of others relating to
race or gender.

*On this day, I will take five minutes to discuss with my child
an item relating to black pride—kente cloth, for instance, or a
family photograph—and suggest
that he let that object inspire him to excellence
throughout the day.*

September 16

VOTING

*People who do not vote have no line of credit with
people who are elected and they pose no threat to
those who act against our interests.*
—*Marian Wright Edelman*

Get the idea? Let's vote! If our children don't see us getting out to the polls, they get the message that they have no stake in things. Dangerous things can happen to a child—to *anyone*—who feels he or she has no voice and no power.

*On this day, I will take five minutes to have a conversation
with my child about voting or about one of our elected officials
and how he or she got into office.*

FATE

Fate is determined by what one does and what one doesn't do.
— *Ralph Ellison*

People can be curiously capricious about the times when they choose to cast "Fate" as the despoiler of their dreams and best intentions. It's fate, we shrug, that we didn't get that job. Is it fate when our child brings home a C-heavy report card?

Our children must never get the notion that life is out of their control. Being born to certain parents and living on a certain block are not indicators of a fate already sealed for them.

On this day, I will take five minutes to talk to my children about choices that they can make in life; and the fact that they can always make changes and improvements; and that any dream can be realized if the will to attain it is strong enough.

September 18

BACKBONE

*If you make yourself into a doormat, people will wipe
their feet on you.*
                                    —*Belizean proverb*

For our children to acquire backbone, it is important
for us to serve as examples. We cannot habitually sacrifice time and space to others when we may need to focus
on our own family's aspirations. It may be difficult for
our child to say no to a friend's particular request, but it
will strengthen our child to stand by choices that are his
own, to value his needs and ideas, and to acknowledge
that people who try to use and abuse us aren't our
friends anyway.

*On this day, I will take five minutes to discuss with my child
the idea of priorities, and that he must resist letting people
knock him off track.*

HATE

Hate is consuming and weakening. Hateful
thinking breeds negative actions.
—Marcus Garvey

Have we made a nest for hatred in ourselves? Allowing
hate to take up space in our lives can make it difficult, if
not impossible, for anything positive to exist inside us.
Hate can be habit-forming. It also provides handy excuses for us not to pursue our goals and find fulfillment.

On this day, I will take five minutes to identify objects of my
hatred and consider whether holding on to these hatreds is
helping me or hindering me from
being the kind of parent I want to be and from
attaining my personal goals.

September 20

CELEBRATION

*The more you praise and celebrate your life, the more
there is in life to celebrate.*
—Oprah Winfrey

Well, we harrumph, Oprah may have a lot to celebrate.
Do *we?*

We cannot afford to make the mistake of rating
our lives according to our degree of material success. It
is not her bank account that causes Oprah Winfrey to
celebrate—although she may indeed give out a little
"Yippee!" when she looks at her checkbook—but the
fact that she is living her dreams and doing the kind of
work that gives her life meaning.

*On this day, I will take five minutes to ask my child what
gives her life meaning, and to encourage her to celebrate what
she finds there now. I will also ask her what she would like to
find there to celebrate in the future, and suggest that it will be
there if she is willing to sweat for it.*

GOALS

One day, after another meet and another loss, I came home and complained to my family that I was tired of losing. I pinned pictures and articles about track and field on a bulletin board in my room, and I started setting goals, writing them down and tacking them onto the board.
—Carl Lewis

Carl Lewis describes these high school goals as "nothing too grand, but they gave me something to shoot for, a time in the 100-yard dash or a distance in the long jump."

We don't have to let our losses defeat us. Like the teenage Carl Lewis, we can use them to motivate us, to become more focused and systematic in approaching our goals, and to drive us to seek inspiration when we need it.

On this day, I will take five minutes to talk to my child about setting goals in some area that interests him.

EXPRESSION

When I was twelve, my mother gave me a diary,
and I would write in that and ultimately in
notebooks and journals. Writing [The Women of
Brewster Place] *did for me what those journals did*
when I was a painfully shy, very troubled teenager.
It got my life in order.
—Gloria Naylor

We don't need to create prize-winning works of fiction for our writing to count. Putting pen to paper can be a great outlet for our stress and can provide a way for our children to express thoughts and feelings they find difficult to share. When we write, we can put things into perspective, blow off some steam, cheer ourselves up, formulate a battle plan, articulate our dreams, and give ourselves encouragement.

On this day, I will encourage my child to start a diary to
express herself and bear witness to the life around her.

FAMILY RITUALS

*What I remember most was an abiding sense of
comfort and security. I got plenty of mothering not
only from Pop and my brothers and sisters when
they were home, but from the whole of our close-knit
community.*
                                        —Paul Robeson

Few of us, these days, have the luxury of extended family or a close-knit community. We have to provide that
comfort by ourselves, whether in tandem with our
spouse or single-handedly.

　　Family rituals or routines can do a lot to make a
child feel secure. There are daily rituals such as a sit-
down family breakfast, a bedtime story, a dinnertime discussion of current events or family news. Weekends
might bring, on a regular basis, a Saturday morning trip
to the library or a family bicycle ride. Sundays can be the
children's turn to prepare a pancake breakfast. And
many find pleasure and comfort in weekly church services.

*On this day, I will take five minutes to think of ways in
which I can create comforting family rituals that suit our
means and temperament.*

COLLECTIVE WORK AND RESPONSIBILITY

*Whether you have a Ph.D., a D.D., or no D, we're
in this together. Whether you're from Morehouse or
No house, we're in this bag together.*
                                    —*Fannie Lou Hamer*

There may be times we feel tempted to disassociate ourselves from the problems of our less fortunate brothers
and sisters. After all, we have our own problems. We get
impatient. We set up play dates for our children only
with the children of parents who seem to have similar
goals and a similar vision for their lives. The fact re-
mains: We and our children face the same uncaring
scrutinizing as all other African Americans. We are all
in this together—and can find joy and satisfaction in
helping each other out.

*On this day, I will take five minutes with my child to discuss
how we can give back to the black community. And then I
will make sure we implement his design.*

MOTIVATION

My father used to work two jobs and still come home
happy every night.
—Magic Johnson

Why did Magic Johnson's father come home happy
every night? One reason might have been that he
looked forward to being with his family. They were the
reason he worked so hard. Of course, there are days of
frustration and/or fatigue, and then—here come the
kids with all their energy, questions, problems, ideas,
and needs. If necessary, let's excuse ourselves for ten or
twenty minutes of "alone time" to pull ourselves together. All but very young children can grasp the notion
that we need their understanding and utmost cooperation. And then, let us attend to our children with joy.

On this day, I will remember that even the most tedious
tasks can be made more bearable by realizing that seeing me
shouldering responsibility will help my children learn what it
takes to be successful in the world.

EXPERIMENTATION

*Childhood experiences, such as having quality
playtime or being allowed to try new and different
things without the fear of being told we're wrong or
stupid, give us permission to be creative and take
risks as adults.*
—Julia A. Boyd

Our children try out new things all the time, just for the
fun of it. It's important not to jump on them with a cri-
tique, which could make them feel inadequate or simply
deflate their pleasure.

Adapting to new situations, accepting challenges,
and taking chances will give them more options as
adults and prepare them for what they will need to do in
order to pursue their dreams.

*On this day, I pledge to allow my child opportunities to
experiment, to stumble, to lose interest, and to excel.*

September 27

SELF-DETERMINATION

*I will not allow one prejudiced person or one million
or one hundred million to blight my life.*
                              —James Weldon Johnson

We must teach our children that they cannot afford to
get bogged down by the prejudice of others. There are always
ways of doing what we want to get done, and always
people who will assist us; we have but to seek them out.
Developing perseverance and a can-do attitude in our
children will help them to function throughout their
lives, no matter the prejudice they encounter.

*On this day, I will take five minutes to talk to my child about
looking within himself to decide who he is, where he wants to
go in life, and how he wants to get there.*

ACTION

It takes too much energy not to care!
—Lorraine Hansberry

It truly does, when you think about it. We hate our current situation, but we learn to numb our feelings, or relieve ourselves of any personal responsibility. We can spend a lot of energy absolving ourselves of the need to act. How much wiser to take the reins and use that energy to rectify the wrongs, and to realize the dreams.

Even in seemingly well-intentioned school systems, our African-American children are being left behind. Do we sit back and accept it? How much energy will *that* require? Better to attend meetings, organize parents, write letters, get involved.

On this day, I will take five minutes to discuss with my child
something that bothers her, and then we will brainstorm
possible actions we might take
to make things better.

September 29

DECISIONS

*Every intersection in the road of life is an
opportunity to make a decision, and at some time I
had only to listen.*
                                            —Duke Ellington

The trick is in realizing that we are indeed at an intersection, and then selecting the most promising direction. As adults, we have generally learned that it does not pay to be impetuous. Our children may be a bit less inclined to stop and take a reading of the situation, so we'll need to guide them as best we can. With time and practice, they will gain confidence in their ability to make the appropriate decision for themselves, and will be less likely to be swayed by the influence of others.

*On this day, I will take five minutes to stop and teach my
child to pause and listen to his heart and mind before
proceeding.*

POTENTIAL

*The potential for strength, endurance, courage,
inventiveness, and creativity exists in every human
being God created.*
                                        —Michele Wallace

It can be hard to see these qualities in our children if we
are unable to see them in ourselves. How can we teach
inventiveness when we ourselves are unwilling to be in-
ventive?

As parents, we must be kind and good to ourselves. We must acknowledge our own potential, find
goals that are meaningful to us, and work for them. It's
good for us, it's good for our children; words ring hollow
when there is no internal commitment to them.

Let us learn to love and honor ourselves. In so doing, we discover our inner resources and learn how to
teach our children how to mine theirs.

*On this day, I will take five minutes to consider if I am
setting a good example for my children by living up to my
own potential.*

COMPLAINING

*I don't have much tolerance for constant
complainers. It's contagious, it's demoralizing, it's
something I really don't want to be around.*
—Dave Winfield

Okay, we all complain once in a while, and our children
are no exception. "Broccoli *again?*" "You never let me
have any fun!"

It can get pretty frustrating. It might help to explain that constant complaints cause us—and others—
to tune out. Also, instead of getting us to listen and,
perhaps, "give in," a steady stream of complaints may
actually cause us to dig in our heels a little more.

Our children need to know that it is good to argue one's point. In my house "negotiation" is encouraged. It doesn't lessen our authority to reverse a decision
once in a while, to let our child "win." But whining is
unacceptable.

*On this day, I pledge to act as an example to my children by
negotiating or in some other way coming up with a plan
when I feel like complaining.*

October 2

TIME

She was an easy mother . . . we seemed always to
have time for ourselves which, I now understand,
was her gift to us.
—Gloria Wade-Gayles

Gloria Wade-Gayles elaborates: "She sacrificed to give us that which she did not have when she was growing up—leisure, emotional space, and education."

We all benefit when we get that time to ourselves. That is when we sift through all the experiences that have an impact upon us, when we contemplate our reactions to them, when we take moral stands, when we grow and dream and plan.

Let's give our children the time they need and permit ourselves the time *we* need for our continued optimal growth.

On this day, I will take five minutes to consider whether I am giving my children and myself enough time for personal growth.

CHALLENGES

*I want to ask you a question. How many of you
have ever thought about something you wanted to do
and you talked you out of it?*
                                        —Les Brown

And if you've done it once, you're likely to have done it
hundreds of times. Can't exercise, you're too busy.
Can't apply for a new job, you're inexperienced. Can't
read more, you're too tired—besides, *Martin* is on.

All right, some of our responses are legit, but often we fall back on the bad habit of rejecting new challenges and dreams. Why? Are we afraid of all the work it
would require, or that we may not have what it takes?
Perhaps we can break things down into a step-by-step
process. Still dubious? Let's just focus on number one
on our list, no further. Then let's talk ourselves into doing something concrete to help us achieve that goal.

*On this day, I will talk to my child about something he
wants to do, and focus on all the ways he can bring himself
closer to achieving it.*

October 4

KNOWLEDGE

*Knowledge is not power, it is only potential power
that becomes real through use.*
— Dorothy Riley

No, it's not enough just to pull A's out of our children
and pack them off to college. Along with pushing an education, we have to push initiative. They have to take
that knowledge and make things happen with it.

Inspired by their dreams and armed with strong
work habits and a commitment to their goals, our children can go out into the world and achieve.

*On this day, I will take five minutes to talk to my child about
the possible ways she might use
the knowledge she has.*

HARMONY

*I have learnt too much of the heart of man not to be
certain that it is only in the bosom of my family that
I shall find happiness.*
—Toussaint L'Ouverture

When we look into the bosom of our own family, what
do we find? Perhaps, at the moment, some conflict or
tension. Entirely normal. It is not an easy order to create a harmonious atmosphere, considering the variety of
personalities and temperaments in a family, all in various stages of the life cycle with different needs and desires. What we *can* do is lay some ground rules so that
individual rights and feelings are respected. We are *all*
obliged to behave in ways that ensure the family as a
pleasant, nurturing "place," but, as parents, *we* set the
tone.

*On this day, I will take five minutes to think about the stress
level in my household, and, if necessary,
ways to reduce that stress.*

FRUSTRATION

*My parents did not encourage me to be bitter. If
they had, I'd have been so mean it would have killed
my spirit a long, long time ago.*
—Annie Elizabeth "Bessie" Delany

Sure, we all have our moments of bitterness, anger, or
despair. It's how we handle these difficult periods that
matters, and this is something we must teach our children. We can become addicted to and enslaved by our
negative feelings—or we can gather all our strength,
support from friends and families, all the optimism and
fight and faith we can muster, and resolve to get past the
bitterness to claim our rewards.

*On this day, I will take five minutes to discuss with my child
things that anger or frustrate us and ways by which we
might channel those frustrations
into improving a situation.*

LEGACY

*Just as a tree without roots is dead, a people without
history or cultural roots also becomes a dead people.*
                                            —*Malcolm X*

What do we teach our children about their family legacy? It is as important for our children to learn about
their great-grandparents who owned a grocery store or
taught school as it is for them to hear of the great civi-
lizations of Africa. They must also learn about our artists, our writers and poets, our thinkers and doctors and
political leaders, who, through industry and determination, overcame tremendous odds to make an impact and
a unique contribution to both our culture and our country.

*On this day, I will take five minutes to discuss with my child
a member of our family or a great man
or woman of African descent.*

FRIENDSHIP

Words are easy, friendship hard.
—Ugandan proverb

By now we have had plenty of experience in the area of friendships. With luck, we can look at our friends and find them a source of support, caring, and humor that we are able to return in kind.

It probably took us a while to figure out who these real friends are, and what the ingredients are that make a friendship meaningful for us. Our children are just beginning to learn. There may be some painful lessons ahead, and while we can try to encourage friendships that will be a positive influence on our child, we won't always be able to spare them the hurt and confusion that childhood friendships bring. What we *can* do is to help our children value and respect themselves, and to think for themselves so they are not misled.

On this day, I will take time to talk to my child about friendships in my life in the hope that he will open up and tell me about his, and sort out his feelings without risk of censure or criticism.

EXCELLENCE

*Don't say, "Hire me because I'm black." Say,
"Hire me because I'm the best. I can deliver and
make you look good."*
—*Anonymous*

Our children must learn that being black matters less
than being able to do the job. Certainly there are many
of us in positions of being able to help our younger
brothers and sisters, but we are powerless to do much
unless they are able to stand on their own merit.

*On this day, I will take five minutes to remind my child that
there are people out there who are happy to help him, but
only if he can deliver the goods.*

ARROGANCE

If tough breaks have not soured me, neither have my glory-moments caused me to build any altars to myself where I can burn incense before God's best job of work.
—Zora Neale Hurston

It happens frequently that an African American of considerable intelligence and wherewithal is made to feel by whites an exception. "You're not like other black people" is the general attitude expressed. It does no good for *any* of us to feel somehow apart from and better than other African Americans.

Let's make sure that, when we tell our child he is so bright and talented, we are not putting across this message that he is better than other black children.

On this day, I will take five minutes to discuss with my child an item relating to black pride—kente cloth, for instance, or a family photograph—and suggest that she let that object inspire her to excellence throughout the day, and to become part of the tradition of excellence of our people.

NURTURING

*My mother thought of human lives as she thought of
the roses that grew in the front yard: sometimes
they wilted, sometimes they almost died; yet with a
"little loving care," a "little gentleness," a "little
concern," those roses always bloomed again.*
—James Thomas Jackson

What do we see when we look at our own garden of loved
ones? There may in fact be some delicate flowers among
hardy specimens, yet each has a unique beauty.

*On this day, I will take five minutes to talk to my child
about nurturing and patience in the cultivation of human
relationships, and to let him know that there is a season for
everything and we should not be discouraged in fallow times.*

October 12

PRIORITIES

One has to find a balance between what people need from you and what you need for yourself.
—Jessye Norman

Even the consummately focused and disciplined opera diva Jessye Norman finds this to be a tricky matter.

At times throughout our lives, we may find ourselves stretched too thin. Perhaps we take on too many commitments and our priorities suffer. We must weed out those things that are diluting our strength or diffusing our focus. Our children, too, may need our guidance with learning how to prioritize. Schoolwork is a top priority, so if sports and other after-school activities begin to take their toll, some rescheduling may be in order.

On this day, I will take time to evaluate my child's priorities, and if they seem to need reorganizing, I will bring up the matter with her.

ACTION

Talk about it only enough to do it. Dream about it only enough to feel it. Think about it only enough to understand it. Contemplate it only enough to be it.
—Jean Toomer

Our child may boast about what he is going to accomplish in life—becoming a millionaire, winning Olympic gold, starting a Fortune 500 company, becoming a celebrated artist—but he must understand that talk is easy; accomplishment takes work.

Our child may argue that he is too young to do anything meaningful toward his ambitions. Not true. If our child plans on becoming an investment banker, he must be able to get into the best schools, which necessitates that he get the best grades *now,* at this very moment. If our child wants to become a respected author, he's got to read, read, read.

On this day, I pledge to stimulate and encourage my child's interests and ambitions, and recognize that what he does now is actually part of the blueprint for his success.

SELF-IMAGE

*There's nothing I'd change about myself. But ask
me again when I'm 25.*
                                    —Beverly Peele

Sure, it's easy when you're a teenage supermodel drawing constant raves and ten thousand dollars a day for
your beauty.

But it's possible our own children feel a tad less
secure when they look in the mirror. Our once-little girl
might suddenly find fault with her changing figure, or
the tooth gap that never bothered her before. Our son
might start feeling unattractively thin when he looks in
the mirror, impatient to fill out. We show our interest
by planning a more healthful diet or scheduling regular
trips to the gym together. A photo of Florence Griffith
Joyner in motion can show our daughter a different kind
of beauty than what she sees in fashion magazines.

*On this day, I will try to be sensitive to my child's
insecurities and, perhaps, offer suggestions on
how she might overcome them.*

October 15

UNITY/BLACK MEN AND WOMEN

*If there is to be a continuum of our struggle for
justice, we must tell our children about great
forerunners. Black women fought side by side with
black men in that movement.*
—*Gil Noble*

Our African-American men and women have always
had a partnership. Yet, these days we're spending a lot of
energy saying, "What's wrong with our men?" or, "The
trouble with black women is . . ."—and the litany goes
on. Our children are growing up with uneasy notions
about their own community, with doubts and generali-
zations.

We need to understand that neither African-
American men nor women can make it alone. Let's stop
pointing at each other and, instead, join hands to give
our children the sense of security and strength they need.

*On this day, I will pledge that, when talking to my
children, I will resist sexist blather and emphasize the fact
that black men and women are in the same struggle and
shouldn't siphon off their energies
by sniping at one another.*

October 16

SUCCESS

*If we dream of our daughters becoming doctors, of
our sons being electrical engineers, we must still love
them when they decide they want to sell shoes and
do landscape gardening.*
—*Viki Radden*

The most and the best we can do is to give our children
as many options as possible. We can nurture a positive
attitude and good study habits, and help them do their
best throughout school so they have their choice of the
finest colleges—but then that's it. We cannot transfuse
our ambitions and dreams into their blood. All we
should hope is that the route they choose for themselves
will bring them boundless fulfillment and gratification—and then we can consider our efforts to have been
a success!

*On this day, I pledge to love my child unconditionally,
to give her guidance, state my own concerns—
then back off.*

VICTORY/DEFEAT

*Too many victories weaken you. The defeated can
rise up stronger than the victor.*
—Muhammad Ali

Sounds contradictory, but it's true: Too many victories
can lead to cockiness and complacency. Of course, we
should applaud our children when they succeed and encourage them to be proud of themselves for succeeding.
We should do nothing to dampen their high spirits during a victory or succession of victories. But there are
times when nothing seems to go right. It is during those
times that we should remind them that in defeat there is
the opportunity to reevaluate strategies, to strengthen
themselves, and to come back stronger than ever.

*On this day I will take five minutes to discuss with my child
something he is having difficulty doing, and encourage him to
locate where the problem is
and how to handle it.*

October 18

LABELING

*I was accused of being a smart mouth, so I became
a smart mouth.*
—Marsha Warfield

We aren't the only ones who label our children. Teachers, friends, and siblings may assign them attributes and appellations kind or unkind, adulatory or hurtful: the thin one, the shy one, the pretty one. In their impressionable youth, it can be too easy for our children to accept the judgment of others, to adopt and conform to outside perceptions of them.

*On this day I will be cautious about the words I use to refer
to my child, realizing that no one label defines her in the
complexity of her evolving and unique self.*

October 19

CONFIDENCE

*Ego is acting like you're all-that. Like they say on
the block, "all-that." Can't nobody touch you.
Confidence is knowing who you are.*
—Shaquille O'Neal

Egotism and confidence—let's not confuse the two
when we look at our own child. The loud brash child
may in fact be masking insecurity. The quiet child we
wish would be a little more extroverted may simply be
perfectly in touch with her own social style.

Our relationship with our child—the way we talk
to her, listen to her, play with her, praise her, and challenge her—can do a lot to fortify that self-confidence. A
simple thing, but so important. Let's make sure our
child knows that we are happy that she is ours.

*On this day, I will take five minutes to think about the
learning and social style of my child and decide whether I
need to step in to boost confidence in certain areas.*

October 20

MISTAKES

Do not look where you fell, but where you slipped.
—Vai proverb

Sometimes we parents are as guilty as our youngsters of focusing on our trip-ups instead of looking further back to determine what contributed to our fall. Seeing only our mistakes and defeats will eventually demoralize us. We may give up, or we may continue blithely on, only to repeat our error. By locating that "crack in the side-walk" that sent us sprawling, we can find ways to either patch it up or sidestep it so that we are more successful in the future.

On this day, I will take five minutes to talk to my child about the importance of learning from your mistakes, recognizing what you did wrong, and applying that to similar tasks in the future.

RESULTS

*I've been fortunate enough to have the opportunity
to make movies, but getting a chance isn't enough.
It's beyond that. I have to produce.*
                                        —Spike Lee

Our children indeed have the opportunity to become
presidents of our country or Nobel Prize–winning scientists, to make the Fortune 500 or to write books that
will become part of the canon of American literature—
why not? To get there, however, they have to produce.
They have to work, remain focused and disciplined, suffer defeat, persevere, and maintain a belief in themselves
and their ultimate success.

*On this day, I will take five minutes to talk to my child about
the importance of getting results.*

October 22

HAPPINESS

*I have this period of happiness here in France, but I
realize that this is a bubble. It's my little bubble. I
think I have earned that, to have an island of
happiness.*
—Elaine Brown

We all deserve to have an island of happiness, but that
does not mean we have to wait 10, 15, 20 years to be
happy. Our "islands" can be part of us now, today. They
are that part of us that give us joy and sustenance, and
we carry them with us throughout our lives. If we do not
work at finding our happiness today, how can we expect
to bump into it years from now?

Let's ask ourselves what brings contentment?
What makes us feel good? Is it writing a poem, playing
chess with our child, volunteering at a hospital or shel-
ter, tending a garden, reading, exercise, entertaining
friends? There are many things that gratify us in different ways. As we experiment, we teach our children that
life offers us many opportunities to find meaning and
pleasure.

*On this day, I will take five minutes to discuss with my child
how he might create his "island of happiness."*

EXPECTATIONS

*We must not only be able to black [shine] boots, but
to make them.*
—*Frederick Douglass*

Our children cannot soar when we weigh them down
with low expectations for their lives. They must be encouraged to dream, and to recognize their dreams as
achievable with diligence and tenacity.

If we constantly snicker at the grandeur of their
fantasies, we are in effect telling them, "Fat chance."
Let's not cause them to doubt their abilities, but encourage them to "think big" when they consider their
lives. As we help them to develop good work habits and
to explore their talents, our children will acquire the
self-confidence required to turn their grandest dreams
into reality.

*On this day, I will encourage my child to talk to me about his
dreams, and be supportive of those dreams, expressing
confidence in his ability to achieve them.*

SELF-DEFINITION

I was a victim; I don't dwell on it.
—Tina Turner

Tina Turner was the victim of physical abuse. Others are victims of poverty, of negligent parents, of various physical and mental handicaps.

Perhaps *we* feel victimized—because of our race, gender, or our socioeconomic status. Are we going to permit feelings of anger, resentment, and helplessness to color our lives forever and limit our potential? Let our children draw from our strength and our sense of personal identity and integrity; these things we yield to no one.

On this day, I will take five minutes to tell my child that we are who we choose to be, and not what others want to make of us.

LOVE

*When I am feeling paralyzed by a task that seems
too difficult, I remember the love that lies at the core
of my family and their legacy to me. The love gives
strength, and I can move again.*
—Jonah Martin Edelman

Here again we see how great a motivator love is. It can
strengthen a child's resolve to do well, to persevere, to
try harder.

But let's turn it around a bit. As much as our
children are strengthened by our love, so are we
strengthened by theirs. That pure and deep affection
can help us through our own times of paralysis to move
forward in pursuit of our dreams.

Full of our children's love, we should never be low
on hope or motivation.

On this day, I will tell my child I love her.

RESTORATION

*Whenever I realize the pace is too nasty, I simply
close the door of myself and sit and listen to God!
He gives me rest and fortifies me for the world.*
—*Pearl Bailey*

We are all entitled to "shut the door" from time to time.
In fact some of us need to do it on a daily basis. Let's
not feel guilty about our miniretreats; they help us to
deal with the children without losing our tempers, to
keep our morale and productivity up in our jobs, to keep
us on top of our crowded schedules.

What feels more restorative? Listening to some
soothing music? A few minutes praying or meditating?
Or relaxing in a fragrant bath after the kids' bedtime?
Why not experiment? Please note: Our children can
"recharge" with some unstructured "downtime" to put-
ter around their rooms, watch the clouds pass overhead,
or simply to daydream.

*On this day, I will take five minutes to discuss with my child
ways in which he might restore himself.*

LIVING FULLY

For this is a beautiful world; this is a wonderful America.
                    —W.E.B. DuBois

Not so wonderful for all of us, admittedly. But we cheat only ourselves when we ignore the physical beauty of America—the lakes, mountains, pastures, oceans, and sunsets. And, granted that America can be politically and socially frustrating for us, we cheat only ourselves when we give way to cynicisim, which often simply paralyzes us.

Let us encourage our children to capitalize on the opportunities available in America. And let us also encourage our children to focus on what America does right, so that we might improve our position and use that new power to correct what America does wrong. That way we further not only themselves, but black people as a whole.

On this day, I will take five minutes to talk to my child about one of his goals and how he might go about realizing it.

FEAR

*Since we are going to encounter scary situations, we
need reinforcement when we do. We need to be aware
that life is scary.*
—Faith Ringgold

We can help our children work through the scary times
if we are sensitive to our children's feelings. Often, the
most important thing we can do is listen. If our child
anticipates our censure or ridicule, he'll be reluctant to
open up. It also helps to figure out the best approach;
our cheerleading style may be inappropriate for the child
who just needs to vent feelings.

We can also try to distract our child with other
activities, to inspire them with books about heroes who
overcame difficulties, or to hold out something fun that
will get the child through the rough stretch. And let's
not overlook prayer and positive thinking.

*On this day, I will make a list of five things I can do with my
child that would help him overcome scary situations—and
pledge not to belittle his fears nor try to pretend that life is
not, sometimes, scary for us all.*

INFLUENCE

*Can't beat the system, so you have to work along
with it. That's what I'm doing.*
—Eddie Murphy

Of course, once we become *part* of the system and have
acquired some power, we can manipulate the system so
that it works for us, too.

If, for example, we feel that our schools are failing
our African-American students, we get involved, go to
school review and PTA meetings, make friends and allies, gather support from administrators, faculty, and
other parents, speak up, organize committees, and force
change.

*On this day, I will take five minutes to think of three things I
can do within my school system to improve it or the way it
works for my child. I will then act on at least one of those
ideas.*

October 30

SEX

*Kids are scared to go to their parents. But kids are
looking for information on how to form good
relationships, how to make wise relations around
sex, and how to have healthy relationships.*
—Linda, 18, who had her first child at 16

We parents can bury our heads in the sand, but our children have urgent problems and need direction and advice. This is especially true when it comes to sex, which for adolescents can be alternately fun, frightening, tantalizing, and forbidden. We need to encourage candid conversations with our children in regard to sex. Granted, *they* might not always be willing, given that volatile mixture of adolescent hubris and angst. But we must do all in our power to let them know they have a safe, nonjudgmental place to turn in the face of peer pressure.

*On this day, I will take five minutes to encourage my child to
be frank with me on an ongoing basis about questions she
might have about sex.*

POLITICS

*Support candidates, run candidates, and retire
candidates.*
>   —Jesse Jackson

We must make our presence felt at the polls.

We do our children, our community, and our
people a disservice if we neglect to become politically
aware and active. We cannot afford apathy; nor can we
afford for our children to adopt a cynical attitude about
their rights and responsibilities as citizens.

It will help for them to learn how to sort out
thoughts, how to make a stand and back it up, how to
respect their own voice, and want to register it officially
on Election Day.

*On this day, I will take five minutes to encourage my child to
discuss political candidates, officeholders,
and issues at home.*

November 1

DETERMINATION

*You could say that race was an obstacle to me, you
could say that sex was an obstacle to me, but I
refused to own them in that way.*
— *Eleanor Holmes Norton*

Have we taken those things that are obstacles to our
gratification and made them a part of us? A shame. If
our obstacle is that we haven't gone to college and we
need to, we can always find ways to get over or around
that obstacle and get ourselves into college. But being
black, or being female are simple facts. If someone has a
problem with those facts, let it remain their problem,
not ours. Let's concentrate on the *real* work at hand.

*On this day, I will take five minutes to talk to my child about
the importance of not being daunted
by the others' opinions, which have no bearing
on our talent or our drive.*

November 2

PROCRASTINATION

There is never time in the future in which we will
work out our salvation. The challenge is in the
moment, the time is always now.
—James Baldwin

How often do we procrastinate? Do our children hear us
going on and on about getting a new job or starting better diet and exercise habits, but never see us commit our
plans to action? The more we put off our goals, the
harder it can get to buckle down to them. Even if we
only take one small step at a time, the forward motion
will help prevent us from feeling stuck in our current situation.

Our children need to learn how to make efficient
use of their time, beginning with study habits. Once
they are used to being adequately prepared, cramming
will seem like an unpleasant prospect.

*On this day, I will take five minutes to consider whether I or
my child have a tendency to procrastinate.*

November 3

ENEMIES

As long as you keep a person down, some part of you has to be down there to hold him down, so it means you cannot soar as you otherwise might.
—Marian Anderson

It takes a lot of energy to keep an enemy. We have to remind ourselves frequently of his treachery, his self-centeredness, or other bad points. We tend to anticipate an assault of some sort, so we keep a wary eye on him. Sometimes we try to seek out allies who will support our view of him, who will take "our side."

So much time, attention, and energy spent! Wouldn't it be smarter to put it all into the effort of making our lives more meaningful and enjoyable?

Our children, too, can get caught up in this grudge keeping.

On this day, I will take five minutes to encourage my child to see that there is more to be gained from positive pursuits, such as making new friends and participating in activities they enjoy, than from grudge keeping.

November 4

DRUGS

Danielle had to spend the first weeks of her life at the
Hospital of St. Raphel in New Haven detoxifying her
mother's methadone from her system.
—from a report in The New York Times

Drug and alcohol addiction hurt not only the abuser,
but also those most intimately connected to him or
her: neglected boyfriend/girlfriend or spouse; parents
and other relatives who must look after the abuser's
children. And in Danielle's case, she not only had to
detoxify methadone, she was born HIV positive.

Whether or not our children are at risk for substance abuse, it is important that they understand the
domino effect such a person has on his own future,
on the lives of his immediate family, and the health
and social fabric of the entire African-America community.

On this day, I will take five minutes to talk to my child
about drug and alcohol abuse and encourage
an ongoing dialogue.

PERSISTENCE

*Wherever I have knocked, a door has opened.
Wherever I have wandered, a path has appeared. I
have been helped, supported, encouraged, and
nurtured by people of all races, creeds, colors, and
dreams.*
—*Alice Walker*

It may take us some knocking and some wandering.
Our knuckles and feet may get sore. Yet, there are people out there who will help and support us in our endeavors.

*On this day, I will take five minutes to talk to my child about
assistance, ideas, and inspiration, and to make sure she
understands that these can come from anyone and from
anywhere.*

November 6

SCHOOL INVOLVEMENT

*Research shows that when parents and teacher have
a good working relationship, the teacher tends to
expect more from a child and to offer her more
encouragement.*
— James P. Comer

Comer, professor of child psychiatry at Yale University's Child Study Center, advises parents to tell their
child's teacher they'd like to stay in touch and ask how
the teacher prefers to communicate. We can also show
our support by volunteering in whatever ways we can—
contributing refreshments to class parties, going along
on class trips, sharing any special expertise or skills with
the class. Every bit we can do counts.

*On this day, I will take five minutes to list ways to
communicate with my child's teacher and ways in which I
can contribute to his classroom. And then I will follow up on
at least one item from each list.*

November 7

BEGINNINGS

However far the stream flows, it never forgets its
source.
—Yoruba proverb

If the source of our stream is polluted and unwholesome, our stream will have a lot to unload along the way.
The force of its current may be lessened.

Let us strive to make our children's start in life a
wholesome and nurturing place. Even if our circumstances at this moment are difficult, we can exert a positive and profoundly meaningful influence upon our
children. Showing our love and fostering self-
confidence and a positive outlook are positive things our
children will carry with them throughout their lives.

On this day, I will take five minutes to consider what I want
to plant at my child's source: laughter,
compassion, resourcefulness?

November 8

PARENTAL JEALOUSY

*My father had always been a symbol of strength
and ability to me. I measured my own talent by his.
But one day you grow up and you surpass your
father.*

—Willie Mays

An interesting experience for a parent—to see our child showing a talent that surpasses our own, whether on the baseball diamond, at the piano, or in the classroom. Yet, no matter our child's age or advanced level of proficiency, let's keep in mind that he or she still very much needs our approbation and support. If we feel a bit jealous of our child's combined youth and talent, we must be extra careful to hold back comments that perhaps unconsciously aim to "take them down a notch." As loving parents, let us exult over our child's gifts, and find it in our heart to encourage him to rise to his full potential.

*On this day, I will compliment my child on at least
one thing he has done.*

November 9

DREAMS

*I believe that you cannot go any further than you
can think. I certainly believe if you don't desire a
thing, you will never get it.*
— *Charleszetta Waddles*

Even today, some of us try to spare our children the anticipated pain resulting from "unrealistic" ambitions by confining their dreams and dampening their desires. With seemingly good intentions some may try to direct them in a certain career path. Yet, to be inspired enough to apply themselves, our children need to be unrestricted in their dreams. Unquestionably, if they aspire to be nuclear physicists, they will feel stifled as computer programmers.

*On this day, I will not encourage mediocrity or "settling,"
but acknowledge that, with enough dedication and hard
work, my child can do anything
and be anything.*

ROLE MODELS

Children have never been very good at listening to their elders, but they have never failed to imitate them.

—*James Baldwin*

What qualities do we hope to find within our children? Well, as parents, we're going to have to do double duty—developing and nurturing these attributes in our progeny and keeping a check on our own behavior to make sure we provide a template of sorts.

If we ask our children to persevere, we cannot be so ready to give up. If we hope they will be disciplined, we cannot be lazy. If we say that reading is important, we cannot spend all our leisure time in front of the tube.

On this day, I will take five minutes to think about what kind of role model I am for my child, and if it needs improvement, I pledge to do that.

November 11

ENVIRONMENTALISM

*My friends know we're going to have to breathe this
air and depend on these oceans and use these trees
just like those upper-middle-class white
environmentalists who most of us tune out even
when they're making sense.*
                                        —*Pearl Cleage*

Dare we talk about saving the world when saving our African-American community seems to drain every last bit of energy? Yet, aren't the two inextricably linked? Can we expect our children to develop intellectually and spiritually in an atmosphere of filth?

We can show our children that their personal actions count. The sense of caring and obligation a child develops as she considers her environment can carry over into other areas of her life, so let's register our commitment and take the lead in attending to the health of our neighborhood, our community, our world.

*On this day, I will take five minutes to talk to my child about
health issues and the environment.*

BLACK PEOPLE

I think black folk are indomitable. In spite of all the
grimness.
                                    —Nathan McCall

Everywhere we turn we are confronted by images of black folk in desperate straits. Yet we're here, and the vigor of our culture is astonishing. Our children have the natural energy and will to succeed; we only have to help them channel it. We need to show them how to create a vision and urge and encourage them to keep it alive through their own efforts.

On this day, I will take five minutes to talk to my child about
one of her goals and how she might
go about realizing it.

PARENTAL INTERACTION

*I noticed, as a child, that my mother got ready for
my father to come home from work. She would put
on a clean dress and comb her hair. I would see
them kiss each other when he came home. It made
me feel very secure and warm.*
                                    —Annette Jones White

How do our children see us relate? Is there more animosity than warmth, more conflict than conversation?
Even for those parents who have separated, every meeting should not be an occasion for unleashing our venom
or turning on the frost.

Our children thrive when there is love and affection. A degree of attitude regulation can benefit any relationship, as well as our personal well-being.

*On this day, I will not be shy about showing affection to the
one I love in front of my child, and to my child.*

VALUES

*I don't care how purdy you is, if you got a bad hawt
you a ugly person.*
                                    —Mance Lipscomb

What values do we teach our children? If our own guid-
ing philosophy is "Beauty conquers all" or "He who has
the most toys at the end wins," then we can't be sur-
prised when our child shows self-centered tendencies.

No question, it is reasonable, admirable, and sensible to want to be physically attractive and lead a comfortable life. But if we neglect to nurture character and
compassion in our children, we fail to promote truly
gratifying and life-enhancing aspects of their lives.

*On this day, I pledge to teach values by example, and be
sure to pass on one of our finest African-American
traditions—"giving back" to the community.*

November 15

STRESS

As a singer, I use songs to keep balance in my life.
—Bernice Johnson Reagon

How do we keep balance in our lives? It makes sense to figure out the antidotes to stress that work best for us, and in so doing start our children on habits that will last a lifetime and improve the quality of their lives. We might try playing the piano, listening to a favorite gospel or jazz artist, going for a run or walk, sketching a still life, weeding the flower bed, stitching a quilt. If we are short on remedies, we can have fun experimenting. It's possible that our friends, relatives, or coworkers can introduce us to new experiences, so let's be open and encourage our mates and children to find their own meaningful outlets.

On this day, I will take five minutes to discuss
with my child or mate things each of us might do
that would allow us to calm down, refuel,
and find our individual center.

CONFIDENCE

*We must nurture our children with confidence. They
can't make it if they are constantly told that they
won't.*
—*George Clements*

It may seem like we'd never consciously set out to un-
dermine our child's ego, but our actions and reactions
can have much the same effect. It may be our show of
impatience when our child is unable to master a new
task on the spot. It may be the disappointment on our
faces when he fails to kick the winning goal, ace the
exam, or become a leader in school. Or it may be all the
unfavorable comparisons to peers or elder siblings we've
made over the years.

    We need to watch what we say as well as what we
convey nonverbally. Our children need to hear and to
believe that we are in their corner and that we have un-
limited faith in them.

*On this day, I will compliment my child on at least one thing
well done, or express, in a more general sense, confidence in
his abilities and intelligence.*

NEED VS. WANT

Necessities never end.
—Kikuyu proverb

Parents certainly know the truth to this one. Our children have absolutely *got* to have this; a week later they cannot *live* without that!

We may have to draw upon our own memories of childhood yearnings, and our sense of humor, too. There will be times we'll want to indulge our child, and times we just have to say, "Sorry, no." Perhaps we'll see the opportunity for our child to work for the object of his desire—through extra chores, or baby-sitting jobs. It can be a valuable experience.

On this day, I will take five minutes to think about an allowance system for my child so that she has her own discretionary money. If I already give her an allowance, I will take five minutes to review it to see if it is adequate and it is being given for the right chores.

November 18

DEFEAT

*Never let your head hang down. Never give up and
sit and grieve. Find another way. And don't pray
when it rains if you don't pray when the sun shines.*
— Satchel Paige

There will be days when our child's head hangs down.
Perhaps he fails to make the team, get invited to the big
party, or make the grade he wanted. There may be little
we can do or say to cheer him up immediately, but it can
help him to know that, out of our defeats, we can pull
the motivation to focus with greater energy on our
goals. That might mean studying harder, practicing
more often—whatever the objective requires.

*On this day, I will take five minutes to talk with my child
about setbacks and defeats; about the fact that it is
how we respond to it that counts.*

November 19

SERVICE

As a Black girl-child, I grew up being socialized to serve—my family, my community, my people. If someone else needed me to do something, it automatically became my responsibility. Now I take suggestions as suggestions and keep them at a distance until I check to see if they are compatible with my own list.
—Bernice Johnson Reagon

Certainly it is a good thing for all of us—men and women—to serve our families and community. But we cannot take all responsibilities upon ourselves.

On this day, I will take five minutes to check preexisting demands on my time and energy before I take on new commitments, and if I am overbooked, I will not hesitate to ask for help from my mate or children if I need it.

November 20

BREAKING CHAINS

*There is in this world no such force as the force of a
man determined to rise. The human soul cannot be
permanently chained.*
—W.E.B. DuBois

Let's look at our children. Have we fettered them with
unfair criticism, harsh words, poor guidance, or low expectations? Have we allowed them to create their own
chains out of fear, cynicism, insecurity, confusion, inappropriate values, or dangerous habits?

Our children's chains, and ours, can and must be
broken. We have to be focused, positive, clever, ener-
getic, and tenacious. We have to resist temptations that
can weaken us and influences that can cause us to give
up. We have to look for inspiration constantly, set
goals, and be systematic in our pursuit of them. We
have to keep ourselves strong, physically and mentally.

*On this day, I will think of ways we as a family can become
a live-in cheering section to support one another as we break
free of the "I can'ts" that hold us down.*

NEGATIVITY

*So many people dwell on negativity and I've
survived by ignoring it; it dims your light and it's
harder each time to turn the power up again.*
—Judith Jamison

A beautiful way to put it! Let's keep our own light bright
so that we always see the way before us. A positive attitude illuminates the hopes and possibilities that are always there if we are resourceful and persistent.

Let's be prepared to shed some light on our children, too, so that they understand that their disappointments should never cheat them of their power.

*On this day, I will compliment my child on at least
one thing he has done.*

ATTENTION

*Even though your kids may not be paying attention,
you have to pay attention to them all the way.*
—*Bill Cosby*

Not only must we pay attention to our children, we must also continue to give them a firm foundation of guidance, values, support, and encouragement.

When our children were babies, we spoke to them with faith that, eventually, they would come to understand us. As they grow older, we must summon up that faith again. Our children may not appear to be paying attention now, but they will have that solid base to draw upon later.

On this day, I pledge to pay attention to my child and not tune him out, so that I don't miss opportunities to lay a strong foundation for a great future.

SELF-IMAGE

Like so many other people, I had to fight feeling ugly. Why as women are we always feeling bad about ourselves?

—Jasmine Guy

It takes one strong self-image to fight the standards of beauty that prevail in our culture. Fortunately, African-American women have, over the years, begun to assert and celebrate their own dramatic range of beauty and style. Regardless, our daughters still fret over being "pretty enough." What can we do?

Her self-image may need bolstering. Let's help her to recognize what it is about herself that makes her proud—the *non*physical attributes. It helps if we've always complimented her intelligence, skills, creativity, resourcefulness, diligence, athleticism, and kindness. A sense of self-confidence will do more for our daughter than any beauty tip. Ditto a strong sense of personal style (how you dress, move, speak, dream, groom, and bejewel yourself). Many a so-called beauty simply possesses a healthy dose of personal style.

On this day, I will tell my children how I think their personal style is beautiful.

EXCELLENCE

Never be the guy who's satisfied to just get by.
—Whitney M. Young, Sr.

Learning to "settle" can be a bad habit that starts young. The child who settles for a B when he could make an A may wind up the adult who settles for an unsatisfying job simply because he is not in the habit of applying himself.

Have we unwittingly sent the message that it's okay to "just get by"? Our habits influence our children. If we embrace challenge, strive for excellence, and encourage our children to do the same, life will hold much greater meaning, pleasure, and gratification.

On this day, I will take five minutes to talk to my child about setting a particular goal in a specific area.

PARENTAL INFLUENCE

Who touches a father touches the son.
—Ethiopian proverb

Let's say our father (or mother) enjoyed spending time with us whenever possible, and helped us feel good about ourselves. It is likely that we will do the same for *our* children. But let's say our parent(s) never knew how to relate to us, ignored our accomplishments, and criticized us frequently. Are we doomed to repeat this sad mistake with our children? A resounding NO!

We may need to work on freeing ourselves from our pasts, but it can be done. Books and magazines on child rearing can be useful sources of information and guidance. We can also observe people who appear to have healthy, accomplished children. Let's give *our* children the parent they deserve!

On this day, I will take five minutes to ask if I am being the best parent I can to my children. If not, I pledge to choose at least one area in which to do better.

QUESTIONS

Philosophy is about the asking of questions.
—Charles Johnson

By asking questions, our children grow—intellectually and emotionally. If we act as though we have no time or interest in their questions, if we ignore them or shush them or our eyes glaze over, or if we respond with sarcasm or mockery, we risk stifling both their curiosity and their powers of critical thinking.

Questions allow our children the opportunity to learn, to clarify issues that confuse them, to challenge the viewpoints of others, to get in the habit of looking for solutions, and to analyze and weigh their options before blindly accepting the answers of others.

On this day, I will take five minutes to discuss something with my children, an item in the newspaper, part of a book that I've read, a snippet of a conversation, a TV news item—and truly discuss it with them, examining it and questioning its premises.

COMMITMENT

*To die for the revolution is a one-shot deal; to live for
the revolution means taking on the more difficult
commitment of changing our day-to-day life
patterns.*
—Frances M. Beal

We have to ask ourselves: Is the way we're living today
getting us where we want to go, or are we just treading
water?

As our people collectively continue the movement
to empower ourselves, each of us wages our own mini-
revolution, which, very simply, is the effort we make to
achieve our goals. If we are not doing anything to move
closer to these goals, we may need to change our daily
patterns.

This goes for our children, too. If their current
study habits are not producing the desired results, we
may need to implement new habits.

*On this day, using family, friends, or historical figures as
examples, I will take five minutes to talk to my child about
the importance of working toward goals
on a daily basis.*

TRADITION/INTEGRITY

*Let our posterity know that we their ancestors,
uncultured and unlearned, amid all trials and
temptations, were men of integrity.*
                                    —*Alexander Crummell*

It was in 1881 that Crummell, a black clergyman, made this plea. Here we are, the "posterity" of which Crummell spoke. Let's make certain that, despite our own trials and temptations, we honor the integrity of our African and African-American forebears by living up to it in thought and deed.

*On this day, I will take five minutes to point out something
to my child, a photograph of a forebear, a patchwork quilt,
my high school yearbook, and tell my child that she is part of
a proud tradition and
that today especially she should bear that in mind
as she goes about her life.*

FAITH

*I am not a quitter. I will fight until I drop. It is just
a matter of having some faith in the fact that as
long as you are able to draw breath in this universe,
you have a chance.*
—Cicely Tyson

One of the perks of being a child is the ability to look to
the future and see it chock-full of opportunity. A child
has little idea of how much hard work and stick-to-itive-
ness it takes to realize opportunity. Unless she is adequately prepared, our child may find it a shock when, on
hitting adulthood, she does not find herself enjoying her
youthful fantasies.

It makes sense to instruct our children in the art
of persevering. Whether it's scoring an A in a difficult
subject or a touchdown on the football field, dedication
is a prerequisite, and that entails having some faith in a
positive outcome.

*On this day, I will teach my child to visualize his success
and to draw upon that vision whenever he needs incentive to
keep trying.*

EXCUSES

Write as well as you rap; teach as well as you dress;
build as well as you dance; study as well as you
condemn others and we will not have to make
excuses.
—Haki Madhubuti

Excuses. Haven't we all made them? We usually know deep down when we're just covering up for a lack of effort, judgment, or perseverance. Excuses ring hollow in our ears.

Given racism, sexism, and the general sorry state of affairs in the world, just what are we going to do? Sit back and cast blame, or secure for ourselves and our families a life of fulfillment and gratification? Writing, teaching, studying, and building all demand our active participation, our effort and energy. The desired results may not come immediately, but along the way we can reap satisfaction that we are contributors to the rebuilding of our people.

On this day, I will take five minutes to talk to my child about channeling energy so that we might become the most productive members of the community that we can be, for a productive life leads to a fulfilling life.

RESILIENCE

*All my work is meant to say, "You may encounter
many defeats, but you must not be defeated."*
—Maya Angelou

We handicap a child when we put across the idea that
life should be smooth sailing, a piece of cake. When our
child bumps up against defeat, he may then get the idea
that it is because of some personal defect, or that he is
not worthy of attaining—or not smart enough or strong
enough to achieve—his goal. One disappointing report
card should not break his academic career!

Far wiser to admit that everyone experiences their
share of rejections and setbacks. It's what we do *after*
them that counts. Our own example is of vital importance. If we are constantly negative, bitter, or depressed
about our lives, our children may adopt our tone and
never find fulfillment or satisfaction.

*On this day, using examples from our family, history or
contemporary life, I will take five minutes to talk to my child
about how we can use our defeats
to fuel us to work harder.*

SPIRIT

*As I look back over my childhood, I realize my
brothers and I were blessed, for we were never
poor—we just didn't have any money. But my
mother saw to it that there was never spiritual
impoverishment in our home or in our lives.*
                                    —George E. Johnson

No doubt about it, lack of money makes everything a
challenge, yet it need not reduce *us* in value. While we
may not be able to afford the material things we'd like
right now, we cannot afford to ignore the riches of the
soul that make all things possible. That spiritual wealth
is the seed money for all our hopes and dreams. Let us
guard it well and invest it wisely.

*On this day, I will take five minutes to consider
whether I am paying enough attention
to the spiritual side of my household.*

STABILITY

I'm secure within myself—independent, a survivor.
—Iman

When we are unstable within, how can we hope to muster the strength to prosper? How do we give our children the foundation they deserve in order to thrive?

Unfortunately, many of us take our fears and insecurities to be a lifelong condition, losing sight of the fact that, through life, we grow, acquire wisdom, and shed past inhibitions and handicaps.

On this day, I will take five minutes to discuss with my child
his victories—the times he has persevered, stood strong,
conquered his fears, and surmounted obstacles.

December 4

ENJOYMENT

My philosophy is very simple. Love yourself. You can do whatever you want to do: sing, cook, dance, write, draw. Whatever your heart desires. Enjoy life, love, and be free.
—Les McCann

Perhaps it is *we* who have made the enjoyment of life so difficult. We ignore simple pleasures. We focus on our burdens and not our blessings. Take children. Our time with them can be enormously pleasurable and satisfying. We can introduce them to our passions (jazz, perhaps?) and ask them to share one of their own with us (say, a book that excites them). Together, we can string cranberries for the tree at Christmas, plant a kitchen garden of herbs, bake some pumpkin bread, sponge paint a family Kwanzaa card.

On this day I will teach my children—and remind myself—that fun comes from our creativity and the effort we put into our daily lives.

December 5

RESULTS

Aiming isn't hitting.
—Swahili proverb

As important as it is to take aim, it is merely an exercise unless we are prepared to follow through. Yes, it may take a number of attempts before we "hit," but the important thing is the willingness to keep trying. This applies to our career efforts, our parenting goals, our fitness regime, our social or intellectual enrichment—any area of our life where we'd like to see change.

On this day, I will take five minutes to discuss with my child concrete ways she can work to achieve her goals.

December 6

BLACKNESS

This is a highly complex world. It can be moved by neither blackness nor beauty. It can only be moved by people who know how to handle power.
—*John Henrik Clarke*

We talk a lot in this book about bolstering our children's self-esteem, which is certainly a factor in an individual's ability to handle power. It shouldn't be a mystical proposition. Getting A's in school is one great way to up self-esteem; as it bestows certain academic credentials upon a student, it simultaneously empowers them. How? It makes our child a "better bet" for prospective colleges, allowing him or her more options and, down the road, opening up more career possibilities.

Yes, it's admirable to promote the beauty in blackness, but let's not overlook the fact that power respects power.

On this day, I will take five minutes to discuss with my child an item relating to black pride—kente cloth, for instance, or a family photograph—and suggest that he let that object inspire him to excellence throughout the day.

STRESS

It's impossible to have total peace, because life isn't like that. You have to take care of yourself.
—Jody Watley

Yes, life is stressful. Our goals change, paths that once looked promising turn into dead ends, people enter and exit our lives with all their energy and expectations. It can only cause more stress to insist on consistent calm.

What we *can* do is stay in top form in order to handle all the challenges to mind and body. This we owe to ourselves, but also to the loved ones who share our lives. How especially unfair to subject our children to our foul moods and snappish tempers.

Proper rest is important. A healthful diet and a commitment to regular exercise will bolster our energy and vitality. Spending time doing things we enjoy, both on our own and with people we enjoy being around, will do wonders for our stress level.

On this day, I will come up with a list of at least five ways I can seek relaxation and release from stress.

December 8

BITTERNESS

*In my early youth a great bitterness entered my life
and kindled a great ambition.*
—*W.E.B. DuBois*

Like DuBois, our children are not immune to bitterness, and race may or may not play a part. A stressful home environment can also do the trick. And not everyone can channel bitterness into ambition.

A watchful parent should be able to spot signs of anger developing. We can help by being available to listen, or by arranging a chat with a counselor or other professional, if necessary.

*On this day, I pledge that, when my child is angry, I will
encourage her to determine what she's upset about and figure
out what she can do about it.*

December 9

EXCELLENCE

*People don't pay much attention to you when you
are second best. I wanted to see what it felt like to be
number one.*
—Florence Griffith Joyner

In order to put their full energy and commitment into
their goals, our children need to feel driven. Agreeing
beforehand to settle for less than their dreams will whit-
tle away at their incentive.

If Florence Griffith Joyner merely aspired to be
somewhere among the top five female runners, she may
never have captured Olympic gold.

*On this day, I will take five minutes to pledge my support to
my children in achieving their own visions of gold and teach
them the inherent pleasure in striving for something
important.*

FULFILLMENT

*People pay for what they do, and still more for what
they have allowed themselves to become. And they
pay for it very simply: by the lives they lead.*
                                        —James Baldwin

If we find our lives currently unsatisfying, let us ask
why. Have we been diligent enough in determining what
would give us a sense of fulfillment? Have we applied
ourselves vigorously to that goal? Perhaps we were
thrown off course by money pressures, romantic losses,
or other factors. We may have lost momentum, but we
cannot afford to give up hope. With ingenuity and flexibility, we can fashion lives of contentment and satisfaction.

*On this day, I will take five minutes to meditate on whether
or not I am satisfied with my life. If not, I will resolve to
better it in specific ways.*

December 11

ENCOURAGEMENT/PUSH

If I came home with a B on my report card, my parents
would praise me for doing well and then suggest that next
time I could come home with an A, if I worked hard enough.
—Jessye Norman

How far do we go in pushing our children to excel? Can
our exhortations to do better backfire?

It depends, certainly, on what we say and the
manner in which we say it. Depends, too, on the child
and the situation. To an underachieving B student, that
push might help, but to a struggling C student that B
should be celebrated for the moment.

Let's always preface our remarks with a pat on the
back. Our children need to hear we're proud of them.
But let us not fear the pursuit of individual excellence.
When we tender our "push" with gentleness and encouragement, we can help our child realize his true potential.

On this day, I will take five minutes to think about the
pressure to excel I am putting on my child. Am I giving him
too much or too little? Just the right amount? Do I need to
adjust according to the endeavor?

EXCUSES

People mistake their limitations for high standards.
—Jean Toomer

Someone who is shy and uneasy with people may turn it around in his mind to say he will not bow and scrape to please other people. We often make excuses for not working through our "limitations." The problem comes when we are held back because we have allowed our limitations to close off certain avenues of opportunity.

Certainly we should not brand our children with labels that can restrict them. It can be too easy for them to feel hampered and to get in the habit of making excuses.

On this day, I pledge to inspire my children, to challenge their perceived limitations, or to find ways to work around them so that they are never tempted to restrict their dreams.

EDUCATION

Education is the jewel casting brilliance into the future.
—Mari Evans

When we regard our children's education as precious, then all our efforts toward safekeeping and polishing will feel less of a burden and more a source of gratification and pleasure. True, there will be frustrations. There will be times we're worn down, stressed out, tired to the bone. Still, we'll need to summon up our energy to attend school meetings and parent-teacher conferences, spend time checking the social studies report, reviewing the math homework, and discussing the latest book our child has read. And when we crawl into our beds we will do so with not just fatigue, but satisfaction over having guarded well the gem that will yield our child a brilliant future.

On this day, I will take five minutes to evaluate how I might support my child better at school and be a more effective advocate for him.

December 14

OPPORTUNITY

*Take advantage of every opportunity; where there is
none, make it for yourself.*
    —Marcus Garvey

Sometimes we are unable to see the opportunities out
there. We forget to look, or we get too busy or too cynical. Our children are the ones who suffer. We may, for
example, note some mathematical aptitude in our
daughter, but assume that tutoring to develop that talent is out of reach financially. An inquiry or two might
turn up a free tutoring program, or scholarship assistance. Or perhaps we can find a teacher who will tutor in
exchange for some resource or talent we have.

*On this day, I will take five minutes to think about
something I would like for my child but that seems out of
reach. I will then brainstorm, perhaps with friends, to come
up with ways I might do it.*

OPTIMISM

*For me, the big issues all come down to the children.
What are we doing to protect them, to make their
future world better?*
—*Janet Jackson*

We must show our children that they have power; they can change and improve things. We do this by being informed voters, by being involved in our schools and communities. As proof of our significance and personal power, we can inform them of their heritage—of all the African Americans who struggled and achieved so that our world today is better than their world was years ago. We can also encourage them to help with humanitarian campaigns—such as contributing food and clothing or soliciting funds for relief efforts—for troubled areas around the world.

Yes, things can get better, and we are the ones who must see that they do.

*On this day, I will take five minutes to consider whether I
am doing all I can to make a better world for my child's
generation, and, if not, I pledge to begin doing so in small
ways today.*

December 16

CONFIDENCE

*Once I get the ball you're at my mercy. There's
nothing you can say or do about it. I own the ball, I
own the game.*
—Michael Jordan

How do we nurture the kind of confidence it takes to
be a champion? As parents, we must be able to take a
hard look at our children and determine whether their
cockiness is just a pose masking insecurity, or whether
there's solid self-esteem there.

Our children develop self-confidence when
they're able to feel good about themselves. We must
help them to explore their interests and talents and resist harsh judgments about their less successful attempts. Let's be careful about how we talk to them,
because our words can demolish their nascent self-
confidence.

*On this day, I will take five minutes to gauge my child's level
of confidence, and to evaluate the general tenor of my
conversations with him—do I spend more time praising or
chastising him?*

PROGRESS

*In knowing how to overcome little things, a
centimeter at a time, gradually, when bigger things
come, you're prepared.*
—Katherine Dunham

It may seem that a marathon lies ahead of us before we
can achieve our most precious goals. We can't become
intimidated. Whether it's a house in the suburbs, a rise
to the top of the corporate ladder, a business of our own,
or a loss of forty pounds, let's remember to take one
step, clear one hurdle, at a time. As we move along, we
pick up confidence, wisdom, and insight, which fortify
us on the way to our goal.

*On this day, I will take five minutes to talk with my child
about the steps she is taking to accomplish
one of her goals.*

December 18

CHARACTER

When the score is zero–zero, you have equal opportunity. But at the end of the game, a red light goes off in one of the dressing rooms and that's the one that seized opportunity and with a combination of effort, and character, and discipline, achieved the victory.

—*Jesse Jackson*

Effort. Character. Discipline. These are the words that turn opportunity into victory. They do not descend on a person from out of the sky. As parents, our duty is to develop these attributes in our children. As parents, we must show them the keys to victory.

On this day, I will list ways in which, by example, I am instilling in my child character traits that ensure victory.

PERSISTENCE

Endurance pierces marble.
—Berber proverb

How easily do we give up? Does one *no* send us scurrying in embarrassment, or cursing the unfairness of life, the narrow-mindedness of people?

Perhaps *no* one explained in our youth how crucial a factor endurance is. Our children need to know. Yes, there will be obstacles—failures, setbacks, and disappointments. We must learn how to move beyond the initial pain to glean information that can be useful to us next time. Perhaps we need to study more, practice longer, vary our approach, or check our timing.

We don't want to spend our lives banging our heads against the wall, hoping it will crumble. Endurance means summoning the will and the energy to try again, making whatever adjustments may be called for and refusing to accept *no* as the last word.

On this day, I will take five minutes to talk to my child about persistence and endurance, perhaps using examples from our family, historical figures, or contemporary achievers.

CREATIVITY

If you stifle someone's creativity, you make that
person dangerous.
—John Singleton

Our children are creative beings. Listen to the stories they tell, look at their drawings, see how absorbed they become in their imaginative play. We are wise to be careful not to quash their creative instincts, because they are key to our child's development. When our child is encouraged to think creatively, she can find solutions, make connections, become *interested* in learning. And let's remember—scientists, mathematicians, and businessmen can have minds as creative as writers or sculptors. It's just a different medium.

Recognizing and fostering our child's creativity will add to her self-esteem. It is an outlet, a means to self-expression, a source of gratification and pleasure. Creativity provides opportunities.

On this day, I will take time to find something my child has
done—a school assignment, a drawing,
a clever remark—and praise him
for his intelligence and creativity.

COMPLAINT

I cannot remember a single complaint from Mother;
her first concern was our needs.
—Marian Anderson

When we feel stressed out, dissatisfied, or frustrated—
and who among us doesn't from time to time—it's not
unthinkable that our feelings take the form of complaints. Sometimes we take it out on the children, who
are simply unfortunate enough to be the only other human beings within radar range. But let's not put unfair
blame on them, or they can start to feel put upon and
resentful or guilty and miserable.

Let's avoid statements that begin, "I'm sick of
the way you . . ." and try to phrase our requests more
constructively, as in, "I especially need your cooperation right now. Would you please clean your room?"

Instead of simply complaining, let's see what we
can do to take positive action.

On this day, I will take five minutes to consider whether, on
the whole, I am as constructive as possible
when I ask my child to do something,
especially when I am exasperated.

DREAMS

If you don't dream, you might as well be dead.
—George Foreman

Perhaps we have given ourselves permission to stop dreaming. We may see ourselves as stuck, locked into position with no time or energy for anything but our current obligations. But lingering in our minds might be that book of poetry we'd still like to write, the notion that we could go back to school or turn our sewing skills into a lucrative quilt-making business.

We need to resist the urge to block out our dreams because they are what keep us going and growing. Let's not use our family as an excuse to stagnate; they will adjust. If our children are to follow their own dreams, let's let them see what it takes.

On this day, I will take five minutes to look at my life and see what dreams I may have deferred, and I will resolve to follow one of those dreams anew.

SPEAKING UP

Mama conceded that I was impudent and given to talking back, but she didn't want to "squinch my spirit" too much.
—*Zora Neale Hurston*

The world is tough, as we parents know, and we want our own dear children to be able to make their way through it with spirit and confidence. That means they'll have to be strong and secure enough to stand up to others and speak their minds. At the same time, they cannot simply be smart alecks or back talkers; they need substance—the intelligence and drive to carry through on their words. That means a bit more preparation on our part, but our children will someday thank us. They will know that when they take a stand, they can deliver.

On this day, I will take five minutes to consider whether I am giving my child the proper balance of discipline (so that she won't be a brat) and confidence (so that she will learn that she has power to stand up for herself).

COURAGE

There is a place in God's sun for the youth "farthest down" who has the vision, the determination, and the courage to reach it.
          —*Mary McLeod Bethune*

Vision. Determination. Courage. A child is not born with a fixed supply of any of these. Vision can be sharpened, broadened. Determination can be mined and boosted. Courage can be practiced and strengthened. *We* have to help.

On this day, I will take five minutes to tell my child that I am confident that he can accomplish anything he puts his mind to. Or, if a specific project is before him, I will tell him that I know he will do a great job.

UNITY

*I feel that the same God-force that is the mother and
father of the pope is also the mother and father of
the loneliest wino on the planet.*
—Dick Gregory

Should the African American who makes $50,000 a
year snub another who makes $14,000 a year? If so,
then he'd better be prepared to be snubbed by the African
American pulling in $100,000 a year.

Elitism divides us. Yes, it makes sense to associate
with other people of power who may be able to help
us, but we must also remember to be willing to help
those who are reaching out to us for help. It is the humane
way to live, but it also makes practical sense; when
our entire community is stronger, we all benefit individually
as well.

*On this day, I will take five minutes to talk with my child
about the things and issues that unite black people.*

SELF-DETERMINATION

*The external givens of life merely set the stage, they
do not provide a script. That script, however, must
be generated from within.*
—*John E. Copage*

Being a black person in America at this moment in time
has certain resonances for all of us, but it does not dic-
tate our personal choices and individual initiative, or define our agenda. We must encourage our children not to
accept external definitions of themselves—whether
from black folk or white, from friends or teachers—but
to look inside themselves to decide who they are. And
when they look inside, they must be generous and loving, appreciative and inspired. Let us help our children
to recognize that they are precious and worthy of achieving their dreams, and that they alone are the authors of
their life scripts. As such, they will never be stuck but
can change direction at any time.

*On this day, I will take five minutes to talk to my child about
looking within herself to decide who she is, where she wants
to go in life, and how she wants to get there.*

December 27

COLLECTIVE WORK AND
RESPONSIBILITY

*The underprivileged are the shyest. They are most
reluctant to reveal that which the soul lives by.*
—Zora Neale Hurston

Dreams. How easily can a child say she wants to be pres-
ident when her shoes are pinching her and there are
holes in her socks? That kind of possibility has to seem
remote to a child whose basic necessities are not guar-
anteed.

Today our Kwanzaa celebration deals with
Ujima, the principle of collective work and responsibility, by which we make the problems of our community
our problems and address them. Let us be as generous as
we can, in whatever ways we can, so that no one in our
community feels too shy to shout their dreams.

*On this day, I will find a black child who is not related by
blood to me and take five minutes to have him or her
articulate his or her dreams. If no flesh and blood child comes
my way today, I will take five minutes to think about ways
in which I can have a positive impact on the lives of children
in my community.*

COOPERATIVE ECONOMICS

*Papa would drag us all the way to Mr. Jones' store
to buy groceries, since Mr. Jones was a Negro. It
was not only inconvenient to shop at Mr. Jones', it
was more expensive. We would say, "Papa, why
can't we just shop at the A&P?" And Papa would
say, "Mr. Jones needs our money to live on, and the
A&P does not! We are buying our economic
freedom!"*
—Sarah Louise and Annie Elizabeth
"Bessie" Delany

Long before Kwanzaa founder Maulana Karenga insti-
tuted the principle of cooperative economics, we African
Americans have been making it a practice to support
our brothers' and sisters' businesses. And if the price is
more expensive than others, we might bring a group of
buyers and ask for a discount!

*On this day, I pledge to take my child to a black vendor and
buy at least one item.*

December 29

PURPOSE

Don't let your address be your destination.
—Corla Wilson-Hawkins

This is what Chicago teacher Corla Wilson-Hawkins tells students in her Recovering the Gifted Child program, which she set up to help children labeled "disruptive" or "learning disabled."

To prepare our own children on their journey toward self-fulfillment, we must help them to pack a sense of purpose and fortitude. They will need a basic map to point them in the direction of their goals, and some common-sense travel tips to help them when the road gets rough.

On this day, I will provide my child with at least one opportunity to build self-confidence. It may be asking for his input in a family decision or complimenting him on something well done or an interesting idea.

December 30

CREATIVITY

*There is a jazzy quality to everything black people
do, a spirit of improvisation and self-creation. It is
part of the African aesthetic.*
                                        —Eric V. Copage

Merely churning out homework by applying the minimum possible effort is never very satisfying. It will benefit our children to realize that there are rewards in being creative, in looking for an unusual and exciting way to do something.

It makes sense to start young, by helping our child to discover the joys and satisfaction of applying himself totally to the job at hand. This promotes a healthy attitude toward work that should last a lifetime. If our children aren't encouraged to push themselves, they may never know what they are capable of accomplishing.

*On this day, I pledge to work with my child on a project and
encourage him to look for ways to make it better by
employing his full imagination.*

INDEX

ABOUT THE AUTHOR

Eric V. Copage has contributed articles to the pages of *The New York Times Magazine,* where he is currently an editor. He was a staff reporter for *Life* magazine and the *New York Daily News* and a music columnist for *Essence* magazine. He has a degree in ethnomusicology and has traveled extensively in West Africa. He is the author of *Kwanzaa: An African-American Celebration of Culture and Cooking* (William Morrow, 1991), *Black Pearls* (William Morrow/ Quill, 1993), and *Black Pearls Journal* (William Morrow, 1993). *Black Pearls* was named Blackboard Non-fiction Book of the Year for 1993.

ABOUT THE COVER

The illustration, created by artist Debra Morton Hoyt, speaks to our desire to have our children reach for the sky, with a firm foundation underneath them, and with the light of inspiration above.

At last, a collection of music to celebrate Kwanzaa!
Kwanzaa music—A Celebration of Black Cultures in Song
(Rounder 2133)

This musical exploration of African and African-inspired cultures features household names such as Aretha Franklin and James Brown, cult figures such as Thomas Mapfumo and Clifton Chenier, as well as Malanthini & the Mahotella Queens, Oumou Sangre, Tabu Ley Rochereau, Clarence "Gatemouth" Brown, Bo Dollis & the Wild Magnolias and music from Haiti, the Bahamas, and Peru. These songs celebrate the seven principles of Kwanzaa.

Eric Copage, the author of *Kwanzaa: An African-American Celebration of Culture and Cooking* and *A Kwanzaa Fable* (Quill/William Morrow), compiled and edited this musical collection with Daisann McLane. Copage is also the author of the best-selling collection of sayings from African and African-American cultures, *Black Pearls*. He is an editor of the New York Times Magazine and the former music columnist for *Essence*.

Available on CD and cassette at finer record and bookstores everywhere. If you have difficulty finding this recording at your local record store, call 1-800-443-4727 for mail order service.

Rounder Records, One Camp Street, Cambridge, Massachusetts 02140 USA
Tel: (617) 354-0700 Fax: (617) 491-1970